FLORIDA

DAILY
DEVOTIONS
FOR
DIE-HARD
FANS

GATORS

Daily Devotions for Die-Hard Fans: Florida Gators
Second Edition © 2009 Ed McMinn

Library of Congress Cataloging-in-Publication Data
13 ISBN Digit ISBN: 978-0-9801749-9-1

Manufactured in the United States of America.

For bulk purchases or to request the author for speaking engagements,
email contact@extrapointpublishers.com.

Go to http://www.die-hardfans.com for information about other titles in
the series.

Cover and interior design by Slynn McMinn.
Edited by Slynn McMinn.

*To Martha Baxter Ortega,
whom God has blessed me
with the great privilege of
knowing*

DAY 1

IN THE BEGINNING

Read Genesis 1, 2:1-3.

"God saw all that he had made, and it was very good" (v. 1:31).

While the official records declare that Florida's first football game was a 6-0 win over Gainesville Agricultural College in 1906, football actually began at Florida in 1899. Well, sort of.

Before 1906, what was to become the University of Florida was located at Lake City and was called Florida Agricultural College. In 1899, student pressure forced the school's board of trustees to reluctantly agree to a football team. An engineering teacher, Professor N.H. Cox, volunteered to be the head coach. The pastor of the Lake City Presbyterian Church and a pair of chemistry professors were his assistant coaches. A squad of 19 players was organized, and a game was arranged with Stetson University, but it never came off. Florida's first-ever football team never played a game.

In 1901, FAC and Stetson finally did meet in the state's first intercollegiate football game. More than 2,000 "wildly excited' fans showed up for the game at the Fairground Race Track in Jacksonville on Nov. 22. In fact, the crowd was standing room only, but that was because they had to stand up: there were no seats.

Stetson won 6-0. FAC's best chance to score was stymied when the squad found itself directly in front of a stump on the edge of the playing field and the ball had to be moved back several yards. The lull killed FAC's momentum, and Stetson held.

FAC played Stetson again in 1902, losing 6-5. After that, football was left in the students' hands and did not "officially" exist until 1906 when FAC moved to Gainesville and became the University of Florida.

Beginnings are important, but what we make of them is even more important. Consider, for example, how far the Gator football program has come since that first season.

Every morning, you get a gift from God: a new beginning. God hands to you as an expression of divine love a new day full of promise and the chance to right the wrongs in your life.

You can use the day to pay a debt, start a new relationship, replace a burned-out light bulb, tell your family you love them, chase a dream, solve a nagging problem . . . or not.

God simply provides the gift. How you use it is up to you. People often talk wistfully about starting over or making a new beginning. God gives you the chance with the dawning of every new day. You have the chance today to make things right – and that includes your relationship with God.

It's the first battle in the game that calls out the best resources, the pluck, the endurance and speed of lusty young manhood.
-- Florida Times-Union *on the 1901 FAC-Stetson game*

Every day is not just a dawn; it is a precious chance to start over or begin anew.

DAY 2

THE WALL

Read Philippians 2:1-11.

"That at the name of Jesus every knee should bow, . . . and every tongue confess that Jesus Christ is Lord" (vv. 10, 11).

The Wall of Florida.

That's what goalkeeper Katie Fraine dubbed five of the 2007 Gator soccer team's most anonymous and most important players. They were the defenders, who understood their importance to the team even though the scorers got the headlines. As Fraine put it, at Florida, "Offense may win games, but defense wins championships."

Defense certainly carried the program to a national title in 1998 when the team incredibly gave up only 17 goals in 27 games. But defense has always been the backbone of the SEC's most successful soccer program. The Gators have never had a losing season, have won better than three of every four matches, and in addition to that national championship have won five SEC championships and eight of the 13 SEC tournaments through the 2008 season. The 2008 team was the first in SEC history to record an 11-0 conference record.

Led by Fraine's Wall of Florida, the 2007 team had a 17-5-3 record, won the SEC, and advanced to the second round of the NCAA tournament. Even for a program built on defense, the 2007 bunch was pretty tough. Fraine said of the team, "We have a lot of big girls in the defensive line, and they're all ready to hit people." As they broke their pre-game huddle, they shouted, "Big and strong!" Senior Shana Hudson summed up the defenders' attitude when she said, "It's always nice to go in there and knock some people down."

When the Gators play soccer, thou shalt not pass through the Wall of Florida.

Perhaps few things in life are more downright terrifying than the notion of being exposed and laid bare for all the world to see. Each of us is our own harshest critic, frequently magnifying or emphasizing our faults, shortcomings, and failures. We assume that if people knew the real person inside our skin, they wouldn't like us. So we build walls to protect ourselves from scorn, rejection, and ridicule. We pose for the outside world while hiding behind a wall that keeps others from seeing who we really are.

While it may be safe behind that wall, it's also lonely there. We are reluctant to love and be loved because that means surrender, knocking down the wall and becoming vulnerable. Even when it's Jesus trying to break through, we resist. But how foolish is that? Jesus already knows all about us – and still he loves us. To love Jesus isn't surrender; it's victory.

When I finally gave my life over to God, that's when joy and happiness entered my life.

-- NFL quarterback Kurt Warner

**We build walls so others won't know us,
but Jesus knows us already and loves us still,
so why keep him out?**

DAY 3

COMEBACK KERWIN

Read Acts 9:1-22.

*"All those who heard him were astonished and asked,
'Isn't he the man who raised havoc in Jerusalem among
those who call on this name?'" (v. 21)*

Kerwin Bell had a pair of gimpy legs, but his arm was just fine. He limped onto Florida Field in 1986 and led the greatest fourth-quarter comeback in Gator history.

Bell threw for 7,585 yards as the Gators' quarterback from 1984 to 1987, but in no game was his leadership more keenly felt than in a game in which he didn't play until the last quarter.

Largely because of Bell's injuries that kept him out of action for a month, the Gators were struggling at 3-4 when they hosted Auburn. They had wins over only Georgia Southern, Kent State, and Rutgers.

The season looked to get longer when Auburn led 17-0 after three quarters. At that point, Coach Galen Hall had no choice; he sent Bell into the game.

"When Kerwin came into the huddle and said, 'We can do it.' Well, they were like magic words to us," receiver Eric Hodges said. Bell promptly led the Gators on a touchdown drive and a drive that netted a 51-yard field goal from Robert McGinty. With 7:10 left, Florida trailed only 17-10. While Gator fans fretted, the Tigers proceeded to chew up most of the clock before giving the ball back to Florida at its 34 with only 1:41 left.

Bell "swiftly and methodically" moved Florida downfield. With 36 seconds left, he hit Ricky Nattiel with a five-yard TD toss. The Gators went for the win with a two-point conversion, and Bell dropped back to pass. When he couldn't find an open receiver, he "limped toward the goal line, at times seemingly dragging his legs. He barely squeezed in" for the 18-17 comeback win.

Life will have its setbacks whether they result from personal failures or from forces and people beyond your control. Being a Christian and a faithful follower of Jesus Christ doesn't insulate you from getting into deep trouble.

Maybe financial problems suffocated you. A serious illness put you on the sidelines. Or your family was hit with a great tragedy. Life is a series of victories and defeats. Winning isn't about avoiding defeat; it's about getting back up to compete again. It's about making a comeback of your own.

When you avail yourself of God's grace and God's power, your comeback is always greater than your setback. You are never too far behind, and it's never too late in life's game for Jesus to lead you to victory, to turn trouble into triumph. As it was with Kerwin Bell and the Gators and with Paul, it's not how you start that counts; it's how you finish.

It has to be one of the finest comebacks ever.
-- Coach Galen Hall after the 18-17 win over Auburn

In life, victory is truly a matter of how you finish and whether you finish with Jesus at your side.

DAY 4

MUDSLINGING

Read Isaiah 1:15-20.

"Though your sins are like scarlet, they shall be as white as snow; though they are red as crimson, they shall be like wool" (v. 18).

Clean clothes can certainly make you feel better; they might even inspire you to a football win.

On Thanksgiving in 1923, an underdog Florida football team met Alabama, which was playing for the championship of the Southern Conference. The Gators weren't exactly slouches with a 5-1-2 record, the only loss to powerhouse Army, but the ties meant they couldn't win the league title.

The game was played at Richwood Field in Birmingham, which was rendered a quagmire by a heavy pre-game downpour. *The Gainesville Sun* said the field "presented a dreary sight. The south corner was a pool of ankle-deep water, a huge strip of sticky clay stretching across the center." Alabama dominated the first half, crossing the Gator ten five times, but the defense surrendered only a single touchdown. Ark Newton's booming punts helped keep Alabama at bay. Despite the wet, slippery ball, Newton had more than one kick of 60 yards in the first half. Florida trailed only 6-0 at the break.

The team then got a boost from a surprise source: clean uniforms. At halftime, the coach, Maj. James A. Van Fleet, ordered the reserves to strip down and hand their clean uniforms over to the muddy, filthy starters. The Gators "came out prancing with a vengeance." They simply blew Alabama away with quarterback Edgar Jones scoring two touchdowns and kicking a field goal. Florida won 16-6, a game that knocked Bama out of the conference title and gave the Gators an early bit of national prominence.

A change of clothes changed the game.

Maybe you've never slopped any pigs, and you may not be a fan of mud boggin'. Still, you've worked on your car, planted a garden, played touch football in the rain, rolled around in the grass with the kids, or endured some military training. You've been dirty.

Dirt, grime, and mud aren't the only sources of stains, however. We can also get dirty spiritually by not living in accordance with God's commands, by doing what's wrong, or by not doing what's right. We all experience temporary shortcomings and failures; we all slip and fall into the mud.

Whether we stay there or not, though, is a function of our relationship with Jesus. For the followers of Jesus, sin is not a way of life; it's an abnormality, so we don't stay in the filth. We seek a spiritual bath by expressing regret and asking for God's pardon in Jesus' name. God responds by washing our soul white as snow with his forgiveness.

An athlete's journey towards perfection is often times paved with mud, blood, sweat, and tears.

— Sarah Will, Paralympic Gold Medal winner

When your soul gets dirty, a powerful and thorough cleansing agent is available for the asking: God's forgiveness.

DAY 5

DREAM WORLD

Read Joel 2:26-28.

"Your old men will dream dreams, your young men will see visions" (v. 28).

When she was eight years old, Marcie Hampton wrote down the great dream of her young life -- and it came true.

On Nov. 8, 1994, Hampton wrote a note to Florida volleyball coach Mary Wise, thanking her for speaking to Hampton's Girl Scout troop. In the note, little Marcie wrote, "I like to play volleyball! My dream is to play for your Florida Gators!"

Well, she did. And, oh, how she did.

Hampton was named Miss Volleyball Florida in 2002 after a high-school career that included two state titles. A bevy of college coaches courted her, but that dream was still in front of her and she followed it, staying home to play in Gainesville.

When she finished her Gator career in 2007, Hampton was one of Florida's best ever. She wound up as the school career leader in attacks and number two in digs. Three times she was All-SEC, and as a senior she made the All-South Region Team.

"Not a lot of people get to live out their childhood dreams," Hampton said as her playing time in Gainesville came to a close. "It's kind of surreal sometimes. Every time I put that jersey on, it's just like, 'Wow, this is really happening. This is really cool.'"

Hampton used her own story to inspire younger fans. "It's kind of cool to tell them you can do what you want to do," she said. "I wanted to be a Gator so bad, and here I am."

Yes, it really happened; Marcie Hampton's dreams came true.

Just like her, you have dreams. Maybe to make a lot of money. Write the great American novel. Or have the fairy-tale romance.

But dreams often are crushed beneath the weight of everyday living; reality, not dreams, comes to occupy your time, your attention, and your effort. You've come to understand that achieving your dreams requires a combination of persistence, timing, and providence.

But what if your dreams don't come true because they're not good enough? That is, they're based on the extremely alluring but extremely unreliable promises of the world rather than the true promises of God, which are a sure thing.

God calls us to great achievements because God's dreams for us are greater than our dreams for ourselves. Such greatness occurs, though, only when our dreams and God's will for our lives are the same.

Your dreams should be worthy of your best – and worthy of God's involvement in making them come true.

Chris Doering (1993-95) lived his dream and it showed.
                                              – Danny Wuerffel

**Dreams based on the world's promises
are often crushed; those based on God's promises
are a sure thing.**

DAY 6

CHEAP TRICKS

Read Acts 19:11-20.

"The evil spirit answered them, 'Jesus I know, and I know about Paul, but who are you?'" (v. 15)

Most college football coaches aren't averse to using a trick play every now and then in a crucial situation in a big game. Steve Spurrier may be the only coach, though, who would use a whole series of them.

He did just that in the 1994 SEC championship game against Alabama. The 9-1-1 Gators were decided underdogs to an undefeated Crimson Tide bunch. Florida fought hard but trailed 23-17 as time grew short in the fourth quarter. That's when Spurrier pulled out a whole bag of tricks.

The trickery all started when quarterback Danny Wuerffel faked an injury, limping off the field. Backup quarterback Eric Kresser came in and surprised the Alabama defense by throwing right off the bat, hitting Ike Hilliard for 23 yards. A healthy Wuerffel came back out and lined the team up in what was known as the Emory and Henry Shift, "a bizarre formation where players line up from sideline-to-sideline along the line of scrimmage." Before Alabama could figure out what was going on, Wuerffel lateraled to Reidel Anthony for another gain.

But Spurrier wasn't through. The Gators lined up in the same mind-blowing formation again and threw a double pass from Wuerffel to Chris Doering to Aubrey Hill. The perplexed Tide could do little when Florida actually ran a "routine" play, a game-winning two-yard touchdown pass from Wuerffel to Doering.

Alabama had one last chance, but the Gator defense was ready for any tricks the Tide might have in mind. An Eddie Lake interception finished Alabama off, and Florida had a 24-23 win and its first-ever back-to-back SEC titles, thanks in large part to a few tricks.

Scam artists are everywhere — and they love trick plays. An e-mail encourages you to send money to some foreign country to get rich. That guy at your front door offers to resurface your driveway at a ridiculously low price. A TV ad promises a pill to help you lose weight without diet or exercise.

You've been around; you check things out before deciding. The same approach is necessary with spiritual matters, too, because false religions and bogus Christian denominations abound. The key is what any group does with Jesus. Is he the son of God, the ruler of the universe, and the only way to salvation? If not, then what the group espouses is something other than the true Word of God.

The good news about Jesus does indeed sound too good to be true. But the only catch is that there is no catch. No trick -- just the truth.

When you run trick plays and they work, you're a genius. But when they don't work, folks question your sanity.

-- *Bobby Bowden*

God's promises through Jesus sound too good to be true, but the only catch is that there is no catch.

DAY 7

SMART MOVE

Read 1 Kings 4:29-34; 10:23-11:4.

"King Solomon was greater in riches and wisdom than all the other kings of the earth. The whole world sought audience with Solomon to hear the wisdom God had put in his heart" (vv. 10:23-24).

Florida coach Charlie Strong planned to have defensive end Jarvis Moss on the sidelines when South Carolina lined up for a 48-yard, game-winning field goal on Nov. 11, 2006, with only eight seconds left to play. Moss, however, begged to be put in, and Strong relented. Smart move, coach.

In what may well be remembered as the biggest play of the 2006 national championship season, Moss blocked the field goal and preserved Florida's 17-16 win over the Gamecocks. Robbie Andreu of *The Gainesville Sun* wrote of Moss' block, "Looking back on Florida's national championship run last season, there is one play that has to be considered *the* play." Wide receiver Jarred Fayson said, "That was the play that changed everything"; it "just fueled our team for the rest of the year." Coach Urban Meyer called the block "a great individual effort by a great performer."

Like most great plays, this one was no accident. "We already knew we were going to block it," said defensive end Derrick Harvey, whom Strong originally wanted in the game. "We already knew we were going to get the push up front." During the timeout before the kick, defensive tackles Ray McDonald and

Steve Harris told Moss "they were going to cave in the right side of USC's line" and give Moss a chance to block the kick. They did and Moss did.

"That was the biggest play I've ever made," Moss said. He got the chance because a coach made a last-minute move that turned out to be pretty smart.

Remember that time you wrecked the car when you spilled hot coffee on your lap? That cold morning you fell out of the boat? The time you gave your honey a tool box for her birthday?

Formal education notwithstanding, we all make some dumb moves sometime because time spent in a classroom is not an accurate gauge of common sense. Folks impressed with their own smarts often grace us with erudite pronouncements that we intuitively recognize as flawed, unworkable, or simply wrong.

A good example is the observation that great intelligence and scholarship are not compatible with faith in God. That is, the more you know, the less you believe. But any incompatibility occurs only because we begin to trust in our own wisdom rather than the wisdom of God. We forget, as Solomon did, that God is the ultimate source of all our knowledge and wisdom and that even our ability to learn is a gift from God.

Not smart at all.

I don't hire anybody not brighter than I am. If they're not smarter than me, I don't need them.

-- Bear Bryant

Being truly smart means trusting in God's wisdom rather than only in your own knowledge.

DAY 8

HOMELESS

Read Matthew 8:18-22.

"Jesus replied, 'Foxes have holes and birds of the air have nests, but the Son of Man has no place to lay his head'" *(v. 20).*

One of college football's greatest spectacles and most enduring traditions is the annual Florida-Georgia game in Jacksonville, but in the early days the game was in effect homeless, wandering about as it sought a place to play.

Everything about the Florida-Georgia game is hotly disputed – even when it began. While Florida doesn't include the game in its official records, Georgia and a team representing itself as the University of Florida met in 1904 in Macon, Ga. Florida officials argue that the game doesn't count because the university wasn't established in Gainesville until 1906.

Florida records do recognize the 1915 game, which really gave birth to the series fans know today. The game was played in Jacksonville at old Barrs Field on a Friday. The mayor declared the day a half-holiday, so folks could attend the game. Rather prophetically, the *Florida Times-Union* declared, "Today promises to mark an epoch in the history of football in this city."

The game moved to Athens in 1916 before being interrupted by World War I and resuming in 1919 at a new venue, Tampa. The teams met in Athens in 1920, and the series lapsed until 1926 with another game in Athens and the 1927 game back in Jacksonville.

The 1928 game was significant in that an undefeated Gator team pasted Georgia 26-6, Florida's first win in the series. The game was played in yet another first-time host city, Savannah. Then it went to Jacksonville, Savannah, Gainesville (host city number six), and Athens before in 1933 the peripatetic series finally found a permanent home in Jacksonville.

Rock bottom in America has a face: the bag lady pushing a shopping cart; the scruffy guy with a beard and a backpack at the interstate exit holding a cardboard sign. Look closer at that bag lady or that scruffy guy, though, and you may see desperate women with children fleeing violence, veterans haunted by their combat experiences, or sick or injured workers.

Few of us are indifferent to the homeless when we're around them. They often raise quite strong passions, whether we regard them as a ministry or a nuisance. They trouble us, perhaps because we realize that we're only one catastrophic illness and a few paychecks away from joining them. They remind us, therefore, of how tenuous our hold upon material success really is.

But they also stir our compassion because we serve a Lord who – like them -- had no home, and for whom, the homeless, too, are his children.

Some people beat up on the homeless for sport.
-- Maryland State Sen. Lisa Gladden.

Because they, too, are God's children, the homeless merit our compassion, not our scorn.

DAY 9

YOUNG BLOOD

Read: Jeremiah 1:4-10.

"The Lord said to me, 'Do not say, 'I am only a child' . . .
for I am with you and will rescue you'" (vv. 7a, 8).

Florida freshman golfer Hannah Yun looked a tad younger than her teammates – and with good reason. She was 15.

Yun was believed to be the youngest NCAA student-athlete in the country when she joined the Gator golf team for the 2007-08 season.

"She's a whiz kid," UF women's golf coach Jill Briles-Hinton said about her.

Yun skipped second grade and graduated from Bradenton Prep Academy in two years by taking extra courses online. Because of her age, she had to receive special clearance from the NCAA to join the powerhouse Gator golf team.

How did her teammates feel about the child in their midst? "She's a very mature 15 year old," senior teammate Tiffany Chudy said. "She's very serious and dedicated to golf." Yun was serious enough and talented enough to crack the lineup of one of the best college teams in the country for the first event she got a chance to play in.

Yun blended in surprisingly well at the huge Gainesville campus. "Most folks don't know I'm 15 until I tell them," she said. She said she "sort of" got used to what she called the "Oh my gosh, you're 15" thing. One problem she faced was that because

GATORS

she was too young to get a drivers license, her parents had to chauffeur her to and from campus every day.

And even though Yun and Briles-Hinton understood the LPGA tour was lurking around to snatch the prodigy away, they also knew they had some time together. LPGA rules stipulate that professionals must be at least 18.

While the media seem inordinately obsessed with youth, most aspects of our society value experience and some hard-won battle scars. Life usually requires us to spend time on the bench as a reserve, waiting for our chance to play with the big boys and girls. You probably rode some pine in high school. You started college as a lowly freshman. You began work at an entry-level position. Even head football coaches learn their trade as assistants.

Paying your dues is traditional, but that shouldn't stop you from doing something bold right away, as Hannah Yun did. Nowhere is this truer than in your faith life.

You may well assert that you are too young and too inexperienced to really do anything for God. Those are just excuses, however, and God won't pay a lick of attention to them when he issues a call.

After all, the younger you are, the more time you have to serve.

You're only young once, but you can be immature forever.
-- Former major leaguer Larry Andersen

Youth is no excuse for not serving God;
it just gives you more time.

DAY 10

NAME DROPPING

Read Exodus 3:1-15.

"This is my name forever, the name by which I am to be remembered from generation to generation" (v. 15).

Is there any greater nickname for a football field than "The Swamp," given to Ben Hill Griffin Stadium at Florida Field by Steve Spurrier? "The Swamp is where Gators live," Spurrier explained. Over the decades, though, quite a few colorful and singular nicknames have been associated with Florida athletics.

For instance, Earl "Dummy" Taylor played almost every minute of every game for five years from 1908-1912. He was once called "the greatest drop-kicker to wear a shoe." For decades, the greatest Florida football team in history was the squad of 1928 with its "Phantom Four" backfield that included quarterback "Cannon-ball" Clyde Crabtree, who passed with either hand effortlessly. Jack "Pee Wee" Forsythe was Florida's first paid football coach (1906-08).

Art "Stump" Wright, a defensive lineman in the 1950s, once missed a game because of lime disease. During pre-game warm-ups, the wet ground soaked the line used to mark the field into his uniform, causing severe burns and landing him in the infir-mary. Jimmy "Mighty Mite" Dunn quarterbacked Florida at 142 pounds. In 1958 he snatched victory from defeat when he went 76 yards for a fourth-quarter TD to beat Georgia. Don't forget Chuck Hunsinger "the Humdinger," an All-SEC receiver in 1948-49.

Quarterback Kerwin Bell (See devotion No. 3.) from Mayo, Fla., was tabbed the Throwin' Mayoan. Because he could play practically every position on the field – and he did play both tight end and fullback in Gainesville (1979-82) -- James Jones early on was labeled "The Franchise."

Nicknames are more than just imaginative monikers slapped haphazardly upon Gator players and coaches. They reflect widely held perceptions about the people named. Proper names do that also.

Nowhere throughout history has this concept been more prevalent that in the Bible, where a name is not a mere label but is an expression of the essential nature of the named one. That is, a person's name reveals his or her character. Even God shares this concept; to know the name of God is to know God as he has chosen to reveal himself to us.

What does your name say about you? Honest, trustworthy, a seeker of the truth and a person of God? Or does the mention of your name cause your coworkers to whisper snide remarks, your neighbors to roll their eyes, or your friends to start making allowances for you? Most importantly, what does your name say about you to God? He, too, knows you by name.

The Florida teams of 1906-07 lacked a nickname, sometimes referred to in print as "Pee Wee's Boys" for player-coach Pee Wee Forsyth.
— Writer Tom McEwen

Live so that your name evokes positive
associations by people you know,
the public, and God.

SPEAK UP

Read Mark 1:21-28.

"News about him spread quickly over the whole region"
(v. 28).

If you're disgusted with all the Heisman overkill, with TV's talking heads blathering about the Heisman trophy all year long, blame Florida's longtime sports information director Norm Carlson.

As the 1966 football season approached, Carlson had a problem. He knew how good his senior quarterback – a guy named Spurrier – was, but he didn't think the rest of the world knew. So what Carlson did single-handedly changed the face of his profession: He launched "one of the greatest promotional campaigns college football had ever known."

The landscape was different then: only three TV networks, no cable, no ESPN, no Internet. Not a single Florida game was televised. So Carlson assembled a highlight film featuring Spurrier's best plays at quarterback, place kicker, and punter and mailed it to more than 500 TV stations. Then each Sunday after a game, he phoned sportswriters and Heisman voters, "filling them in on Spurrier's latest exploits." He led a campaign to increase the number of Heisman voters from the South.

Carlson even got the governor, Haydon Burns, involved. Burns was a big Gator booster who volunteered his help in spreading the word about Spurrier. He secured the services of the state tourism department to send out 500 additional film clips that featured Spurrier's highlight plays from the 1966 season.

Spurrier won the Heisman in a landslide, and college football analyst Beano Cook knew why. "To win the Heisman Trophy without being on national TV is like winning the presidential election without winning California," Cook said. "Without Norm, Spurrier doesn't win the Heisman Trophy."

Norm Carlson got the word out.

Commercials and advertisements for products and services inundate us. Turn on your computer: ads pop up. Watch NASCAR: decals cover the cars and the drivers' uniforms. TV, radio, newspapers, billboards -- everyone's trying to get the word out the best way possible.

Jesus was no different in that he used the most effective and efficient means of advertising he had at his disposal to spread his message of salvation and hope among the masses. That was word of mouth. In his ministry, Jesus didn't isolate himself; instead, he moved from town to town among the common people, preaching, teaching, and healing. Those who encountered Jesus then told others about their experiences.

Almost two millennia later, nothing's really changed. Speaking to someone else about Jesus remains the best way to get the word out, and the best advertisement of all is a changed life.

It's sad that the Heisman has become all about the hype.
– blogger on The New York Times *College Sports Blog*

**The best advertising for Jesus is word of mouth,
telling others what he has done for you.**

DAY 12

IN REMEMBRANCE

Read 1 Corinthians 11:23-26.

"Do this in remembrance of me" (v. 24b).

On Sept. 18, 1999, defensive end Alex Brown played against the Tennessee Volunteers, the defending national champions, as though he was a man inspired. And so he was – inspired by a memory.

Brown is one of the greatest defensive players in Florida history. He was three times All-SEC from 1999-2001. He was All-America and the SEC Defensive Player of the Year in 2001. He set the Florida career sack record with 33.

But never was he better than that night against second-ranked Tennessee his sophomore season. He sacked Vols quarterback Tee Martin five times in the 23-21 win that stretched the Gators' home winning streak to 30.

Brown's special night was driven by two reminders written on his left wrist: the initials of two lost friends, Barry Gardner, his high school football coach at Hamilton County High, and McArthur Zanders, a cousin. Gardner had died the previous June of a heart attack; Zanders had died in 1994 in an accident when he fell asleep at the wheel along a country road in Jennings.

"McArthur was older than I was," Brown recalled. "I wanted to be just like him," especially in the way Zanders dedicated himself to football, training on his own before formal practices even started. "When I think about McArthur, I try to make the most of every play," said Brown. "We made a deal that if he didn't make it to the NFL, then I would. He can no longer do that, so it's up to me."

Alex Brown remembered – and he made it to the NFL.

Here's a news flash: One day you will die.

With that knowledge in hand, you can get busy and make some preparations for that fateful day by selecting a funeral home, purchasing a cemetery plot and picking out your casket or opting for cremation and choosing a tasteful urn, designating those who will deliver your eulogy, and even making other less important decisions about your send-off.

What you cannot control about your death, however, is how you will be remembered and whether your demise leaves a gaping hole in the lives of those with whom you shared your life or a pothole that's quickly paved over. What determines whether those nice words someone will say about you are heartfelt truth or pleasant fabrications? What determines whether the tears that fall at your death result from heartfelt grief or a sinus infection?

Love does. The love you give away during your life decides how you will be remembered at your death.

I don't want my children to remember me as a professional football player. I want them to remember me as a man of God.
– Reggie White

How you will be remembered after you die
is largely determined by how much
and how deeply you love others now.

DAY 13

SUPERSTITION

Read 1 Samuel 28:3-20.

"Saul then said to his attendants, 'Find me a woman who is a medium, so I may go and inquire of her'" (v. 7).

You might think the Gators beat Ohio State 84-75 on April 2, 2007, for their second straight national championship because of Joakim Noah, Al Horford, Corey Brewer, Taurean Green, Lee Humphrey, and company. Nah. The credit really belongs to lucky shirts and chicken and rice.

Florida grad Ryan Weinstein found himself in a panic the day of the 2006 championship game in Indianapolis. He had been to ten restaurants and couldn't find any chicken and rice with ranch dressing, his pre-game meal. In desperation, he went to a Chinese place for the chicken and rice and then bought some ranch dressing from Subway. His tenacity paid off with the win over UCLA. Weinstein tried to give up his superstition in 2007, and the Gators promptly lost two straight games. So in Atlanta on championship game day, he scouted area restaurants and found some chicken and rice with ranch dressing.

Scott Frey wore his lucky Gator hat to the championship game along with the same t-shirt and sneakers he wore to Indianapolis. His wife and he left Gainesville for Atlanta at the same time they had departed for Indy even though it meant arriving in Atlanta about 4:30 a.m.

Jordan McDonald also has a secret weapon: his Gator-orange

Sperry Topsiders. He isn't sure why they work; he just knows they do. "I would have driven back [from Atlanta to Gainesville] to get them," McDonald said, "or had them overnighted if I'd forgotten them." Paul Cruz always wore the same blue sweatshirt to the pre-game practices he never missed.

You just can't be too careful, you know.

Black cats are right pretty. A medium is a steak. A key chain with a rabbit's foot wasn't too lucky for the rabbit. And what in the world is a blarney stone? About as superstitious as you get is to say "God bless you" when somebody sneezes.

You look indulgently upon good-luck charms, tarot cards, astrology, palm readers, and the like; they're really just amusing and harmless. So what's the problem? Nothing as long as you conduct yourself with the belief that superstitious objects and rituals – from broken mirrors to your daily horoscope –can't bring about good or bad luck. You aren't willing to let such notions and nonsense rule your life.

The danger of superstition lies in its ability to lure you into trusting it, thus allowing it some degree of influence over your life. In that case, it subverts God's rightful place.

Whether or not it's superstition, something does rule your life. It should be God – and God alone.

I don't believe in a jinx or a hex. Winning depends on how well you block and tackle.

-- Shug Jordan

**Superstition may not rule your life,
but something does; is it faith in God?**

DAY 14

THE BREAKFAST CLUB

Read Genesis 9:1-7.

"Everything that lives and moves will be food for you. Just as I gave you the green plants, I now give you everything"
(v. 3).

Imagine being told to eat as much as you can possibly consume so that you can gain as much weight as you possibly can!

That's the situation for The Breakfast Club, but it's not exactly the most fun in the world for a group of Florida football players who are regular club members. They gather faithfully and hungrily at 7:30 every Tuesday morning in the Gator Dining Hall under the watchful eyes of strength and conditioning coordinator Mickey Marotti.

Their mission? To pack on the pounds, to make them bigger football players.

Their means? Eating as much food as they can stomach -- and then a little more. "Eggs, pancakes, whatever makes you put on pounds," said Duke Lemmens, a freshman in 2007 who was undersized for the defensive line at 240 pounds.

It isn't as much fun as it may sound. After weeks of practically having food forced down his throat, Lemmens said that eating really isn't enjoyable anymore. "We don't really like it," he said. "It makes me not want to eat anymore."

Sophomore receiver David Nelson was another member of this unique group; in 2007 he carried only 200 pounds on his lanky

6-foot-5 frame. "If there's something we should have that we don't have, [Marotti] makes us go get it [or he] brings it to us and we have to eat it," Nelson said.

But what if you're full to the point you're miserable? "If you can't eat it, you still have to eat it."

Belly up to the buffet, boys and girls, for barbecue, sirloin steak, grilled chicken, and fried catfish with hush puppies. Rachael Ray's a household name; hamburger joints, pizza parlors, and taco stands lurk on every corner; and we have a TV channel devoted exclusively to food. We love our chow.

Food is one of God's really good ideas, but consider the complex divine plan that gets those French fries to your mouth. The creator of all life devised a system in which living things are sustained and nourished physically through the sacrifice of other living things in a way similar to what Christ underwent to save you spiritually.

Whether it's fast food or home-cooked, everything you eat is a gift from God secured through a divine plan in which some plants and animals have given up their lives.

Pausing to give thanks before you dive in seems the least you can do.

All we gave by way of scholarships were meals at Ma Rainey's and rooms to the top players who could not afford it.
– Florida head coach Charley Bachman (1928-32)

God created a system that nourishes you through the sacrifice of other living things; that's certainly worth a thank-you.

DAY 15

ATTITUDE CHECK

Read 1 Thessalonians 5.

"Give thanks in all circumstances, for this is God's will for you in Christ Jesus" (v. 18).

At the time, Steve Spurrier's years as head coach were, according to Peter Kerasotis, "the most sensational and memorable era in UF football history. For the Florida Gators, it was their days of Camelot. Twelve years produced six Southeastern Conference championships, one national championship, 122 victories, and "unprecedented success and national exposure" done "without even the hint of cheating."

So what did Spurrier inject into the program that awakened the dormant giant that was Florida football when he arrived in January 1990? What monumental changes did he make that put the Gators on top and have kept them there through the Urban Meyer regime? It's probably not what you think.

What he changed was the Florida attitude. "What Florida needed," Spurrier said, "was just a lot better attitude than we'd had in the past. . . . There's some principles and guidelines that winners have, and I just tried to instill those in the team. Fortunately, all the guys bought into it. . . . We had the attitude to keep playing no matter what happens."

Linebacker Jerry Odom, who later became an assistant coach on Spurrier's staff, was present at Spurrier's first-ever meeting with his Gator team. "He was telling us we were going to win,

GATORS

that we were going to beat Auburn, that we were going to beat Georgia, that we were going to be champions. It was just an attitude, and he made you believe."

It was indeed "just an attitude," but it made all the difference in the world for the Gators -- and it's still making a difference.

How's your attitude? You can fuss because your house is not as big as some, because a coworker talks too much, or because you have to take pills every day.

Or you can appreciate your home for providing warmth and shelter, the coworker for the lively conversation, and the medicine for keeping you reasonably healthy.

Whether life is endured or enjoyed depends largely on your attitude. An attitude of thankfulness to God offers you the best chance to get the most out of your life because living in gratitude means you choose joy in your life no matter what your circumstances.

This world does not exist to satisfy you, so chances are it will not. True contentment and joy are found in a deep, abiding relationship with God, and the proper way to approach God is not with haughtiness or anger but with gratitude for all he has given you.

I became an optimist when I discovered that I wasn't going to win any more games by being anything else.
-- Earl Weaver

Your attitude determines more than your mood; it shapes the kind of person you are.

DAY 16

THE SURE FOUNDATION

Read Luke 6:46-49.

"I will show you what he is like who comes to me and hears my words and puts them into practice. He is like a man building a house, who dug down deep and laid the foundation on rock" (vv. 47-48).

Florida is today one of the nation's premier college football programs, but it wasn't always that way. A coach whose overall record wasn't that good laid the foundation for today's success in football and in all sports.

Many of the early days in Florida football history were "filled with an overabundance of optimism on the part of the alumni and dreams that could easily be shattered." But then, "Mark this, and mark it well," wrote Fred Pettijohn of the *Fort Lauderdale News.* "Starting with his first season at Florida, . . . Bob Woodruff started building a solid foundation under Florida football."

Woodruff came to Gainesville in 1950, and though his record (53-42-6) was rather mediocre, he "push[ed] the Gators from the bottom into the upper-division" of the SEC. In 1952, he guided the Gators to their first-ever bowl appearance, a win over Tulsa in the Gator Bowl.

Woodruff's efforts off the field laid the foundation for the university's overall athletic future. Doubling as the athletic director, he took a number of "bold steps aimed at bringing the entire Gator athletic family to the top of the SEC." Among his shrewdest moves was a doubling of the capacity of Florida Field to 44,000. This drastically increased the athletic department's revenue and meant that for the first time Florida could play its home games in Gainesville rather than traveling around the state to larger stadiums. As Woodruff said later, the expansion "made the entire sports program go."

The foundation was laid for the success that was to come later.

Like Florida's entire athletics program, your life is an ongoing project, a work in progress. As with any complex construction job, if your life is to be stable, it must have a solid foundation, which holds everything up and keeps everything together.

R. Alan Culpepper said in *The New Interpreter's Bible*, "We do not choose whether we will face severe storms in life; we only get to choose the foundation on which we will stand." In other words, tough times are inevitable. If your foundation isn't rock-solid, you will have nothing on which to stand as those storms buffet you, nothing to keep your life from flying apart into a cycle of disappointment and destruction.

But when the foundation is solid and sure, you can take the blows, stand strong, recover, and live with joy and hope. Only one foundation is sure and foolproof: Jesus Christ. Everything else you build upon will fail you.

Jesus Christ is the rock upon which I stand.

-- Danny Wuerffel

In the building of your life, you must start with a good, solid foundation in Christ, or the first trouble that shows up will knock you down.

DAY 17

GOOD TIMES

Read Revelation 21:1-7.

"There will be no more death or mourning or crying or pain, for the old order of things has passed away (v. 4b)."

To put it mildly, Gator gymnastics coach Rhonda Faehn had a good week.

Faehn took over in May 2002 as the program's sixth coach. She brought with her from the University of Nebraska experience at the highest levels as a member of the 1988 U.S. Olympic Team and an All-American gymnast at UCLA. She saw at Florida "a program with the potential to firmly establish itself among the nation's elite." That vision has become a reality with the Gators now among the nation's top ten every year and always in the discussion when possible national champions are discussed.

Faehn, therefore, has had some good times since she arrived in Gainesville. Nothing, however, could top the week she had in January 2008. On Tuesday, Jan. 8, she gave birth to her first child, which was certainly pretty good for starters. She was still in the hospital when the Gators opened their season with a win over Illinois-Chicago. Assistant Adrian Burde's wife provided an anxious Faehn with constant text message updates during the meet.

So what happened? The squad posted the highest season-opening score in school history, which catapulted the Gators into the No. 1 ranking in the nation. When she returned to practice on

Monday, Faehn had a new son and the nation's top-ranked team. Her gymnasts welcomed Faehn back with a group hug. "I think she had tears in her eyes because she was so excited to be back and to see us," junior Corey Hartung said.

"I couldn't have asked for more," the coach said about her extraordinary seven days.

Good times don't last. You may laugh in the sunshine today, but you know that sometime – maybe tomorrow -- you will cry in the rain. That knowledge and that certainty drive many to lose their lives and their souls in alcohol and drugs and a lifestyle devoted to the frenetic pursuit of the good times, a frantic and doomed effort to outrun the bad times lurking around the corner.

The pursuit of the good times isn't necessarily the problem. Rather, it's the places where we seek them that condemn us to failure and despair. The good times the world provides are inevitably temporary, which means we soon must begin the vicious cycle again.

Only when we quit chasing the good times and instead seek the good life through Jesus Christ do we discover an eternity in which the good times will never end. In Jesus, the fruitless hunt ends; the fruitful living begins.

My life isn't good because I'm a football player. I'm a football player because my life is good. Jesus Christ has made my life good.
                                    – NFL quarterback John Kitna

Let the good times roll—forever and ever for the followers of Jesus Christ.

DAY 18

TEAM PLAYERS

Read 1 Corinthians 12:4-13; 27-31.

"Now to each one the manifestation of the Spirit is given for the common good" (v. 7).

Understandably, a weight room is all about getting bigger, stronger, and tougher. At Florida, though, it's also about getting closer as teammates.

Mickey Marotti's offseason conditioning program for Gator football players is legendary. The director of strength and conditioning, Marotti is in essence the acting head football coach once May arrives since head coach Urban Meyer and his staff by NCAA rules can have only limited contact with the players.

Not so Marotti. He's with them at 6:30 a.m. for the morning runs, and then come the one-on-one mat drills and the lifting sessions in the weight room. It's there that Marotti teaches the Gators – of all things – chemistry.

Particularly in the spring of 2008 did Meyer and Marotti feel that building a strong bond among the players was important. That's because the coaches saw that the 2007 team, which had a bunch of freshmen and only a few seniors, was not very close coming off the 1996 national championship. "I've seen a lot of chemistry develop," Marotti said, "but they have to do it off the field, maybe hanging out and eating together."

Sophomore center Maurkice Pouncey could see the difference. "We're like a big family," he said. "I'm glad we're all closer."

"My whole thing is maturity and the chemistry," Marotti said. "If you've got those two things, I think you're heading down the right path. I think that's where we're heading."

Those Gators kept right down the path all the way to another national championship, one that began with the development of muscles and teammates in the weight rooms.

Most accomplishments are the result of teamwork, whether it's a college football team, the running of a household, the completion of a project at work, or a dance recital. Disparate talents and gifts work together for the common good and the greater goal.

A church works exactly the same way. At its most basic, a church is a team assembled by God. A shared faith drives the team members and impels them toward shared goals. As a successful Gator football team must have running backs and offensive tackles, so must a church be composed of people with different spiritual and personal gifts. The result is something greater than everyone involved.

What makes a church team different from others is that the individual efforts are expended for the glory of God and not self. The nature of a church member's particular talents doesn't matter; what does matter is that those talents are used as part of God's team.

Celebrating team goals with teammates is a lot better then celebrating all by yourself on some podium.
  — Danny Wuerffel after the 1997 Sugar Bowl win over FSU

**A church is a team of people using their talents
and gifts for God's glory rather than their own.**

DAY 19

AMAZING!

Read: Luke 4:31-36.

"All the people were amazed and said to each other, 'What is this teaching? With authority and power he gives orders to evil spirits and they come out!'" (v. 36)

It is getting so you can't figure football no more."

So spoke Florida assistant head coach Gene Ellenson after one of the most amazing victories in Gator history. On Nov. 27, 1965, Florida trailed FSU 17-16 with 73 seconds left to play. The Gators won 30-17.

A pair of Steve Spurrier touchdown passes to Jack Harper, one for 52 yards and the other for 37, put Florida up 13-3 at halftime. When Wayne Barfield kicked a 34-yard field goal in the third quarter to make it 16-3, the Gators were coasting.

But the Seminoles mounted a ferocious comeback. They scored twice, the last TD coming with only 2:10 left on the clock, and took a 17-16 lead. The kickoff didn't help the Gators much, forcing them to start from their own 29. Spurrier hit Charlie Casey for ten and Harper to the Seminole 43. Another completion to Casey netted another first down, this one at the 25.

Spurrier then scrambled and had a wide open field in front of him, but instead of running, he motioned Casey to retreat into the end zone. He did and Spurrier hit him for the touchdown. Barfield's extra point made it 23-17 with 73 seconds left.

The amazing turnaround and the Florida Field pandemonium continued when Allen Trammell intercepted a pass with 19 seconds left and took it 46 yards to finish the Noles. Florida had scored twice in 54 seconds.

"It was certainly the finest victory of my career," Coach Ray Graves said after the game. And the most amazing.

The word *amazing* defines the limits of what you believe to be plausible or usual. The Everglades, the birth of your children, Krispy Kreme donuts, your spouse's love for you, those last-second Gator wins -- they're amazing! You've never seen anything like that before!

Some people in Galilee felt exactly the same way when they encountered Jesus. Jesus amazed them with the authority of his teaching, and he wowed them with his power over spirit beings. People everywhere just couldn't quit talking about him.

It would have been amazing had they not been amazed. They were, after all, witnesses to the most amazing spectacle in the history of the world: God himself was right there among them walking, talking, teaching, preaching, and healing.

Their amazement should be a part of your life too because Jesus still lives. The almighty and omnipotent God of the universe seeks to spend time with you every day – because he loves you. Amazing!

It's amazing. Some of the greatest characteristics of being a winning football player are the same ones it's true to be a Christian man.

-- Bobby Bowden

Everything about God is amazing,
but perhaps most amazing of all is that he loves us
and desires our company.

DAY 20

MAKING PLANS

Read Psalm 33:1-15.

"The plans of the Lord stand firm forever, the purposes of his heart through all generations" (v. 11).

Offensive coordinator Fred Pancoast had a plan he was so sure of that before a game he declared exactly when Florida would score its first touchdown.

All-American defensive end Jack Youngblood recalled that Pancoast stood up and told the team, "We are going to score on the third play of the game." Youngblood remembered that his attitude was "Right, right." He had good reason to be skeptical; everybody else was.

The game was the 1969 season opener against the Houston Cougars. The season before they had set an NCAA record by averaging 568 yards a game. *Playboy* had made them its preseason No. 1. The media dubbed the Cougars "football's greatest show." Even the locals weren't too optimistic; a headline previewing the game declared "There's Just No Way."

But Pancoast had a plan. He also had a pair of sophomore surprises waiting for the Cougars: a gunslinging quarterback named John Reaves and a fleet-footed receiver named Carlos Alvarez. On the first play, the Gators ran up the middle as they had done for most of the 1968 season. On the second play, they did the same. On the third play, Reaves faked the run and hit Alvarez in stride for a 70-yard touchdown, just as Pancoast had planned it.

Houston never recovered. By halftime, Florida led 38-6 and thousands of Gator fans were streaming into Florida Field "to witness the second half of this incredible upset." Florida won 59-34 as Reaves set school records for passing yardage, touch-down passes, and total offense.

The plan worked.

Successful living takes planning. You go to school to improve your chances for a better paying job. You use blueprints to build your home. You plan for retirement. You map out your vacation to have the best time. You even plan your children -- sometimes.

Your best-laid plans, however, sometimes get wrecked by events and circumstances beyond your control. The economy goes into the tank; a debilitating illness strikes; a hurricane hits. Life is capricious and thus no plans -- not even your best ones -- are foolproof.

But you don't have to go it alone. God has plans for your life that guarantee success as God defines it if you will make him your planning partner. God's plan for your life includes joy, love, peace, kindness, gentleness, and faithfulness, all the elements necessary for truly successful living for today and for all eternity. And God's plan will not fail.

If you don't know where you are going, you will wind up somewhere else.

-- *Yogi Berra*

Your plans ensure a successful life;
God's plans ensure a successful eternity.

DAY 21

GOD'S WORKFORCE

Read John 15:12-17.

"I chose you and appointed you to go and bear fruit --
fruit that will last" (v. 16).

He wasn't playing much and he was devastated. But he didn't quit, he didn't whine, he didn't complain. He just went to work and became part of University of Florida basketball legend.

Joakim Noah enjoyed only limited playing time as a freshman in the 2004-05 season. In Florida's first-round NCAA tournament win over Ohio University, for example, he didn't play at all. Coach Billy Donovan described Noah as "completely devastated. He was so competitive and passionate and wanted to play."

Noah decided that sitting on the bench had to end, so the morning after his freshman season ended, he was in the weight room working out with assistant coach Larry Shyatt. "The people who work the hardest are the ones who usually make it, you know, at this level," Noah said in explaining his regimen. "Jo is a worker," Donovan said. "He's one of the first guys in the gym every day and one of the last ones to leave."

The work paid off. Noah played in every game over the next two seasons as the Gators amassed 68 wins and won back-to-back national championships. He led the team in blocks both seasons, finishing third on the Florida career list. He was the leading scorer for the 2006 champions and scored more than 1,000 points in the two seasons. In the 2007 draft, he was taken in the first round by

the Chicago Bulls, the ninth overall selection.

The coaches "just told me to keep working," Noah recalled about his disappointing freshman season. He did -- and Gator fans will be forever grateful.

Do you embrace hard work as Joakim Noah does or try to avoid it? No matter how hard you may try, you really can't escape hard work.

Funny thing about all these labor-saving devices like cell phones and laptop computers: You're working longer and harder than ever.

For many of us, our work defines us perhaps more than any other aspect of our lives. But there's a workforce you're a part of that doesn't show up in any Labor Department statistics or any IRS records.

You're part of God's staff; God has a specific job that only you can do for him. It's often referred to as a "calling," but it amounts to your serving God where there is a need in the way that best suits your God-given abilities and talents

You should stand ready to work for God all the time, 24-7. Those are awful hours, but the benefits are out of this world.

With hard work, anything's possible.
— 2006 football national championship game defensive MVP
Derrick Harvey

God calls you to work for him using the talents
and gifts he gave you; whether you're a worker
or a malingerer is up to you.

DAY 22

UNDERDOG

Read 1 Samuel 17:17-50.

"David said to the Philistine, . . . 'This day the Lord will hand you over to me, and I'll strike you down'" (vv. 45-46).

He was truly "a little guy among the giants," someone who would never line up at running back in a game for the University of Florida -- but there he was.

He was Tim Higgins, all 5-foot-7, 162 pounds of him, an undersized walk-on who never really expected to play a down but who kept putting on the pads at practice, taking hit after hit, and doing whatever he could to make the Florida Gators a better football team. Coach Urban Meyer was so impressed with Higgins' effort and selflessness, he put him on scholarship in 2006. "I saw a little guy who did everything we asked him to do," Meyer explained.

But even Higgins wore down sometimes. "There were times when I was frustrated," he said. "I always believed God had a plan for me, but sometimes I wondered why I was here."

He wondered no longer after Nov. 18, 2006, when Florida destroyed Western Carolina 62-0 on its way to the national championship. In a scene reminiscent of the movie *Rudy* (though unlike Rudy, Higgins had no trouble getting into Florida; he was a National Merit Scholar), the fans began to chant Higgins' name. "People were screaming, 'Give me Higgins!'" Meyer said. "So I gave them Higgins."

He sent Higgins in at running back rather than his natural position, wide receiver, so he could touch the football. Tim Tebow, who outweighed his new tailback by almost sixty pounds, "had to line me up because I didn't know where I was going."

Higgins was stopped for no gain, but it didn't matter. David had conquered Goliath again.

You probably don't gird your loins, pick up a slingshot and some smooth, round river rocks, and go out to battle ill-tempered giants regularly. You do, however, fight each day to make some economic and social progress and to keep the ones you love safe, sheltered, and protected.

Armed only with your pluck, your knowledge, your wits, and your hustle, in many ways you are an underdog; the best you can hope for is that the world is indifferent. You need all the weapons you can get.

How about using the ultimate weapon David had: the absolute, unshakable conviction that when he tackled opposition of any size, he would prevail. He knew this because he did everything for God's glory and therefore God was in his corner. If you imitate David's lifestyle by glorifying God in everything you do, then God is there for you when you need him. Who's the underdog then?

Always remember that Goliath was a 40-point favorite over Little David.

-- Former Auburn coach Shug Jordan

Living to glorify God is the lifestyle of a champion.

DAY 23

SWAMP FEVER

Read 1 Corinthians 6:12-20.

*"Do you not know that your body is a temple of the Holy
Spirit, who is in you, whom you have received from God?
. . . Honor God with your body" (vv. 19, 20b).*

A swamp is hot and sticky and can be dangerous." It doesn't
sound like a place you'd want to visit, but Florida fans know it as
a field of dreams.

Steve Spurrier added a new twist to legendary Ben Hill Griffin
Stadium at Florida Field when he christened it "The Swamp"
after the 1991 season. "There is no better place than 'The Swamp,'"
ESPN's Lee Corso once declared, but it took decades of hard work
and dedication to create the most exhilarating and exciting site in
all of college football.

With an original capacity of 21,769, Florida Field was constructed
in 1930. The visionary for the stadium was school president John
Tigert, who saw something more than the "water-filled sinkhole"
on which the facility was built. Construction cost $118,215.80
and took only seven months. More than 20,000 fans christened
the new facility on Nov. 8, 1930. It consisted of the lower half of
the current stadium. In 1934, the stadium was dedicated to the
memory of the servicemen who died in World War I.

Since that 1930 dedication, Florida Field has seen many mile-
stones. The first of many expansions was in 1950, also the year the
first night game was played, a 7-3 win over The Citadel. Expan-

GATORS

sions in 1965 and 1982 raised the capacity to 72,000. The stadium was renamed Ben Hill Griffin Stadium at Florida Field in 1989, and further expansions raised the capacity to more than 90,000.

For the Gators and their fans, only the best home field will do, even if it is a swamp.

While you may feel that you, too, deserve only the best when it comes to your personal playing field, you may not see a field of dreams when you look into a mirror. Too heavy, too short, too pale, too gray — there's always something wrong because we compare ourselves to an impossible standard Hollywood and fashion magazines have created, and we are inevitably disappointed.

God must have been quite partial to your body, though, because he personally fashioned it and gave it to you free of charge. Your body, like everything else in your life, is thus a gift from God. But God didn't stop there. He then quite voluntarily chose to inhabit your body, sharing it with you in the person of the Holy Spirit.

What an act of consummate ungratefulness it is then to abuse your God-given body by violating God's standards for living. To do so is in fact to dishonor God.

If you don't do what's best for your body, you're the one who comes up on the short end.

-- Julius Erving

**You may not have a fine opinion of your body,
but God thought enough of it
to personally create it for you.**

DAY 24

DANCE THE NIGHT AWAY

Read 2 Samuel 6:12-22.

*"David danced before the Lord with all his might, while
he and the entire house of Israel brought up the ark of the
Lord with shouts and the sound of trumpets" (vv. 14-15).*

Danny Wuerffel was witness to some "questionable dancing"
by a certain well-known Gator during his 1996 Heisman-Trophy
weekend in New York.

The whirlwind of activities in the Big Apple included a fund-
raising, black-tie banquet, after which Wuerffel and his family
and friends returned to the Downtown Athletic Club. When the
musician in the lounge took a break, Wuerffel sat down at the
piano. "Normally, I'm not so bold," he said, "but, hey, I'd just won
the Heisman Trophy and I was the man of the hour."

His mom, who, Wuerffel said, chose to invest her beautiful
voice in singing in the church rather than a professional career,
came up and added a professional voice to his melodies, starting
off with "Unchained Melody." Before long "the entire lounge was
rocking with George Rogers (the former Heisman Trophy winner
from South Carolina) and my mom singing 'Lean on Me' while
everybody in the place swayed and sang along."

That wasn't the only music during the gala weekend. A smaller
banquet the night before included former Heisman winners and
their families. Wuerffel described it as "a fun night of great food,
good music and questionable dancing."

Included in that dancing was the rather startling sight of coach and former Heisman winner Steve Spurrier doing his version of the Macarena with Wuerffel's sister. Just how questionable was the dancing? As Wuerffel put it, "After witnessing the Macarena episode, let me just say this about Coach Spurrier as a dancer: He's a tremendous play-caller."

One of the more enduring and unfortunate stereotypes of the Christian is that of a dour, sour-faced person always on the prowl to sniff out fun and frivolity and put an immediate stop to it. "Somewhere, sometime, somebody's having fun – and it's got to stop!" Many understand this to be the mandate that governs the Christian life.

But nothing could be further from reality. Danny Wuerffel and his family, Steve Spurrier, George Rogers – devout Christians all – demonstrated pointedly to the non-believers in their midst that the Christian life is all about celebrating, rejoicing, and enjoying God's countless gifts, including salvation in Jesus Christ.

If anybody on God's green earth has reason to dance and sing, it is Christians. Yes, music can be obscene and dancing can be vulgar, but the Christian life turns upon what is in the heart.

To dance, to sing, and to live for Jesus can't be anything but beautiful.

Dancers are the athletes of God.

– Albert Einstein

While dancing and music can be vulgar and obscene, they can also be inspiring expressions of abiding love for God.

DAY 25

TOLD YOU SO

Read Matthew 24:15-31.

"See, I have told you ahead of time" (v. 25).

If anyone could ever have said, "I told you so," it would have been Jack Youngblood.

He played linebacker for Jefferson County High in Monticello, which had only about twenty players on the team. The team won the 1966 Class B state title, but because the school was so small, nobody was scouting Youngblood.

Well, one scout from Florida State – Tallahassee was only 25 miles away -- did come to see Youngblood play, an assistant coach whose evaluation of football talent would improve with experience: guy named Bill Parcells. And Parcells' assessment of Youngblood? He told FSU Coach Bill Peterson that Youngblood would never play college football.

One coach finally noticed. After the state championship game, "We were hooting and hollering and jumping all over the place," Youngblood recalled. "This guy grabs me." He was Dave Fuller, the Gator baseball coach, who helped with football recruiting. He offered Youngblood a scholarship, which he accepted on the spot. It was not as though he had a number of options. "I had planned on going to North Florida Junior College. Florida was my one and only offer," Youngblood said.

The opinion of Bill Parcells and all those college coaches who ignored Youngblood notwithstanding, the rest is glorious football history. In 1970, Youngblood was the SEC Lineman of the Year, All-SEC, and All-America. He was selected to the All-Time SEC Team in 1983. He played defensive end for the Los Angeles Rams for 14 seasons and was inducted into the Pro Football Hall of Fame in 2001.

Jack Youngblood can tell them all, "I told you so."

Don't you just hate it in when somebody says, "I told you so"? That means the other person was right and you were wrong; that other person has spoken the truth. You could have listened to that know-it-all in the first place, but then you would have lost the chance yourself to crow, "I told you so."

In our pluralistic age and society, many view truth as relative, meaning absolute truth does not exist. All belief systems have equal value and merit. But this is a ghastly, dangerous fallacy because it ignores the truth that God proclaimed in the presence and words of Jesus.

In speaking the truth, Jesus told everybody exactly what he was going to do: come back and take his faithful with him. Those who don't listen or who don't believe will be left behind with those four awful words, "I told you so," ringing in their ears and wringing their souls.

There's nothing in this world more instinctively abhorrent to me than finding myself in agreement with my fellow humans.

-- Lou Holtz

**Jesus matter-of-factly told us what he has planned:
He will return to gather all the faithful to himself.**

DAY 26

PRESSURE COOKER

Read 1 Kings 18:16-40.

"Answer me, O Lord, answer me, so these people will know that you, O Lord, are God (v. 37).

When it came right down to clutch time, Florida's national champion men's basketball team of 2006-07 could handle the pressure.

Nowhere was that more evident than in the two games leading up to the Elite Eight in the 2007 NCAA Tournament. The Gators made it through not just because they were selfless, coachable, and talented -- which they were -- but also because they were all of those things when the game was on the line.

On Sunday, March 18, 2007, the Gators' response to pressure was downright amazing. Purdue was playing tough, and with only four minutes left to play, the game looked like a buzzer beater. Instead, Florida won by scoring on every possession, making some stops on the defensive end, and controlling the backboards. The result was a 74-67 win without a nail-biting finish.

"We made some key plays," Coach Billy Donovan said. Indeed. *The Gainesville Sun* said, "Whether it's the big-game experience or the maturity factor or the fact that these guys are just good, they are still playing because they have come to play at the right times." "When your back's against the wall, we know we have to make a play," Corey Brewer said.

Against Butler the following Friday, the Gators demonstrrated that clutch time isn't always in the last four minutes. Butler led by nine in the first half, but the Gators responded with their usual aplomb. They went on a 17-2 run to complete the half; Butler didn't make a field goal in the last 8:42.

The Gators won 65-57 and were on their way to the Elite Eight -- and the national championship -- because they were able to do whatever it took when the pressure was the greatest.

You live every day with pressure. As Elijah did so long ago, you lay it on the line with everybody watching. Your family, coworkers, or employees -- they depend on you. You know the pressure of a deadline, of a job evaluation, of taking the risk of asking someone to go out with you, of driving in rush-hour traffic.

Help in dealing with daily pressure is readily available, and the only price you pay for it is your willingness to believe. God will give you the grace to persevere if you ask prayerfully.

And while you may need some convincing, the pressures of daily living are really small poatoes because they all will pass.

The real pressure comes in deciding where you will spend eternity because that decision is forever. You can handle that pressure easily enough by deciding for Jesus. Eternity is taken care of; the pressure's off. Forever.

Pressure is for tires.

-- *Charles Barkley*

**The greatest pressure you face in life
concerns where you will spend eternity,
which can be dealt with by deciding for Jesus.**

DAY 27

SHOUT! SHOUT!

Read Psalm 100.

"Shout for joy to the Lord, all the earth!" (v. 1)

Awash in color and noise."

That's how Danny Wuerffel said it felt to come out of the tunnel in the south end zone onto Florida Field on game day. So many people shouted so loudly it was "one of the most surreal things you can imagine," like entering "another world, another dimension, where reality ended and a cartoon-like universe began." The noise was "all around you, beneath you, beside you and above you."

Should the Gators be greeted and supported any other way? Shouldn't Florida Field be the noisiest place in the universe when the Gators play? Shouldn't all Gator fans everywhere shout themselves hoarse whether they're at the game, watching on TV, or listening to the radio?

The spontaneous yells of the crowd aren't the only element of what Wuerffel called the "greatest environment in all of college football." The synchronized shouts such as "Go Gators" add to the bedlam. History records that the fabled Gator war cry probably originated back in 1907 when Neal Storter made the team. Because Storter came from a town in the Everglades, other players naturally associated him with alligators. They nicknamed him Bo Gator.

GATORS

The story goes that Storter saw only limited playing time because he was too slow, but in one game he recovered a fumble and took off downfield. Knowing who was on the loose, the crowd let loose with a mass cry of "Go Gator!" The battle cry was born. (History also records that Storter didn't score on the play despite the cheer.)

Perhaps there are times other than a Florida game when you've acted not quite like the sane, reserved, and responsible person you really are. The birth of your first child. Your wedding day. The concert of your favorite band. That fishing trip when you caught that big ole bass. You've probably been known to whoop it up pretty good when your emotions get the best of you.

But how many times have you ever let loose with a powerful shout to God in celebration of his love for you? Though God certainly deserves it, he doesn't require that you walk around waving pompoms and shouting "Yay, God!" He isn't particularly interested in having you arrested as a public menace.

No, God doesn't seek a big show or a spectacle. A nice little "thank you" is sufficient when it's delivered straight from the heart and comes bearing joy. That kind of shout carries all the way to Heaven; God hears it even if nobody else does.

The Swamp rocked like never before, a din of noise that probably set off car alarms in the parking lot.

-- Sportswriter Pat Dooley

The shout of joy God likes to hear is a heartfelt "thank you," even when it's whispered.

DAY 28

PROMISES, PROMISES

Read 2 Corinthians 1:16-20.

"No matter how many promises God has made, they are 'Yes' in Christ" (v. 20).

Tim Tebow made three promises -- and the 2008 college football season was never the same again.

On Sept. 27, Florida's season apparently crashed and burned with a stunning 31-30 loss at home to Mississippi. The upset devastated Tebow, and "for an hour after the loss [he] sat in silence in front of his stall." At one point, Coach Urban Meyer joined him by sitting on the floor next to him for a while without saying a word.

But Florida's third Heisman-Trophy winner didn't need the moral support; he was not just despairing. He was preparing himself, marshalling not just his remarkable talents but also his incredible resiliency and the strength he finds in his faith. He was getting ready for the rest of the season.

When Tebow left the locker room and strode to a lectern to meet a gaggle of reporters, the rest of the season had begun for him. And he made The Promises:

"You have never seen any player in the entire country play as hard as I will play the rest of the season.

"You'll never see someone push the rest the rest of the team as hard as I will push [the Gators] the rest of the season.

"You'll never see a team play harder than we will the rest of the season."

Austin Murphy of *Sports Illustrated* called Tebow's promises "a jaw-dropping moment of accountability." The result was "a galvanized bunch of Gators who went on a tear for the ages."

The march to the 2008 national championship had officially begun.

The promises you make don't say much about you; the promises you keep tell everything.

The promise to your daughter to be there for her softball game. To your son to help him with his math homework. To your parents to come see them soon. To your spouse to remain faithful until death parts you. And remember what you promised God?

You may carelessly throw promises around, but you can never outpromise God, who is downright profligate with his promises. For instance, he has promised to love you always, to forgive you no matter what you do, and to prepare a place for you with him in heaven.

And there's more good news in that God operates on this simple premise: Promises made are promises kept. You can rely absolutely on God's promises. The people to whom you make them should be able to rely just as surely on your promises.

In the everyday pressures of life, I have learned that God's promises are true.

-- Major leaguer Garret Anderson

God keeps his promises just as those who rely on you expect you to keep yours.

DAY 29

A DOG'S LIFE

Read Genesis 6:11-22; 8:1-4.

"God remembered Noah and all the wild animals and the livestock that were with him in the ark" (v. 8:1).

As unlikely as it may sound, a dog had a hand in a Gator victory over Georgia in Jacksonville.

Chuck Hunsinger is one of the greatest runners in Florida football history. He was All-SEC in both 1948 and 1949. Against Alabama in 1948, he scored on a five-yard pass reception, a 77-yard run, and a 96-yard kickoff return, a performance that inspired a veteran sportswriter to write a song about him called "Hunsinger the Humdinger."

Heading into the 1949 game against the hated Bulldogs, the Gators had lost to Georgia seven straight times. Needless to say, Florida fans were pretty sick of losing, and one true Gator fan decided to give Hunsinger a little extra incentive. If Hunsinger liked anything better than running with the football, it was hunting with a good bird dog. So Gator fan Al Hearin promised Hunsinger that he would give him one of the best bird dogs in the country if he would score two touchdowns in the first half against Georgia.

Duly inspired, Hunsinger went out and did indeed score twice in the first half. He then added a third TD in the last half to pace a 28-7 pasting of Georgia. Hearin made good on his promise, handing the Humdinger a beautiful dog worth $500. Mindful of the role the offensive line played in providing him the holes through which he exploded, Hunsinger named his new bird dog "Blocker."

Not only did Hunsinger get the dog, but he got the award: SEC Back-of-the-Week for his performance against Georgia.

Do you have a dog or two around the place? How about a cat that passes time staring longingly at your caged canary? Kids have gerbils? Maybe you've gone more exotic with a tarantula or a ferret.

Americans love our pets; in fact, more households in this country have pets than have children. We not only share our living space with animals we love and protect but also with some – such as roaches and rats – that we seek to exterminate.

None of us, though, has the problems Noah faced when he packed God's menagerie into one boat. God saved all creatures from extinction, including the fish, who were probably quite delighted with the whole flood business.

The lesson is clear for we who strive to live as God wants us to: All living things are under God's care. It isn't just our cherished pets that God calls us to care for and respect; it's all of his creatures.

I like dogs better [than people]. With people, you never know which ones will bite.

-- Diver Greg Louganis

**God cares about all his creatures,
and he expects us to respect them too.**

DAY 30

ONE THING FOR SURE

Read Romans 8:28-30.

"We know that in all things God works for the good of those who love him, who have been called according to his purpose" (v. 28).

That Florida attempted a field goal to win the 1966 Auburn game was no surprise. That Steve Spurrier was the kicker *was* a surprise, so much so that in the record Florida Field crowd that afternoon probably only Spurrier, Florida Coach Ray Graves, and one other person knew the kick was a sure thing.

With a little more than two minutes left to play, the score tied at 27, and Florida's undefeated season on the line, a Gator drive stalled at the Auburn 24. "It was a frustrating game because we were really a lot better than them," Spurrier said.

Graves was ready to send in field goal kicker Wayne Barfield when Spurrier went over to the head coach, pointed at himself, and said, "Let me have a shot at this one." Graves agreed without hesitating though Spurrier had not attempted a field goal since the season opener. The coach recalled, "I had heard before the game that Steve told some of the players during breakfast that he dreamed he kicked a field goal to beat Auburn."

Spurrier nailed it. "No doubt," he recalled. "I kicked it right in the middle of the goalposts." The dramatic 30-27 win undoubtedly clinched the Heisman for Spurrier, who with his coach knew he would make it.

GATORS

But who was that other person who knew it was a sure thing? Auburn Coach Shug Jordan. When Spurrier trotted onto the field for the kick, his assistant coaches didn't believe he would kick it, shouting to the players to watch for the fake. Jordan said to them, "You better hope it's a fake, because if Steve Spurrier tries this field goal, he will make it."

Football games aren't played on paper. That is, you attend a Florida game expecting the Gators to win, but you don't know for sure. If you did, why bother to go? Any football game worth watching carries with it an element of uncertainty.

Life doesn't get played on paper either, which means that living, too, comes laden with uncertainty. You never know what's going to happen tomorrow or even an hour from now. Oh, sure, you think you know. For instance, right now you may be certain that you'll be at work Monday morning or that you'll have a job next month. Life's uncertainties, though, can intervene at any time and disrupt your nice, pat expectations.

Ironically, while you can't know for sure about this afternoon, you can know for certain about forever. Eternity is a sure thing because it's in God's hands. Your unwavering faith and God's sure promises lock in a certain future for you.

There is nothing in life so uncertain as a sure thing.
-- NHL coach Scotty Bowman

Life is unpredictable, and tomorrow is uncertain;
only eternity is a sure thing --
because God controls it.

DAY 31

DECIDE FOR YOURSELF

Read John 6:60-69.

"The words I have spoken to you are spirit and they are life. Yet there are some of you who do not believe" (vv. 63b-64a).

Otis and God -- that's all Tim Tebow had with him when it came time to make the biggest decision of his life. Turned out it was more than enough.

On Dec. 13, 2005, time was running out. The deadline Tebow had established for deciding which school he would play football for had arrived. Florida seemed a lock; after all, the mailbox at the Tebow farm boasted a Gator helmet, and a Gator shower curtain hung in his bathroom. But Tebow and Alabama Coach Mike Shula had established a personal connection during the recruiting process, so the decision came down to Alabama or Florida.

Though they were Gator fans to the core, Tebow's parents let their son make the decision. "We kept all the calls away and gave Timmy the day to think about it," Tim's mother, Pam, said. "The [farm's] lake is a real boys' place. It [is] a good place to think."

So Tebow cut off the outside world completely by retreating with Otis, the family's golden retriever, to that lake. There he sat on the bank next to Otis, thought things through, and prayed for a sign from God. In the end, he said, he went with his heart. He just knew he wanted to be a Gator.

Two years later, Tebow recalled, "It really was a hard decision. I grew up loving the Gators, but that didn't automatically mean Florida would be the right fit for me. . . . I found out that it was and now I couldn't be happier. There's no better place than right here."

The decisions you made along the way shaped your life at every pivotal moment. Some decisions you made suddenly and frivolously; some you made carefully and deliberately as Tim Tebow did when it came to choosing a college; some decisions were forced upon you. Perhaps decisions made for frivolous reasons have determined how your life unfolds, and you may have discovered that some of those spur-of-the-moment decisions have turned out better than your carefully considered ones.

Of all your life's decisions, however, none is more important than one you cannot ignore: What have you done with Jesus? Even in his time, people chose to follow Jesus or to reject him, and nothing has changed; the decision must still be made and nobody can make it for you.

Carefully considered or spontaneous – how you arrive at a decision for Jesus doesn't matter; all that matters is that you get there.

This decision has not been made hastily, but thoughtfully and prayerfully.
-- Ray Graves, announcing his decision to become Florida's athletic director

A decision for Jesus may be spontaneous or considered; what counts is that you make it.

FLORIDA

KEEP OUT!

Read Exodus 26:31-35; 30:1-10.

"The curtain will separate the Holy Place from the Most Holy Place" (v. 26:33).

The Hula Bowl, a college all-star game, told Cris Collinsworth thanks but no thanks – we don't want you.

Collinsworth is one of Florida's greatest players. From 1978-1980, he was three times an All-SEC wide receiver, and in 1980 he was an Associated Press second-team All-America. He went on to a professional career that included being named to the Pro Bowl three times and playing in two Super Bowls.

Collinsworth came to Florida as a quarterback, and in the first game of his college career, he set a school record that will never be broken. Against Rice he was the back-up quarterback, and in one sequence he rolled right from the Gator one and hit a wide open Derrick Gaffney. Gaffney went 99 yards to complete the longest touchdown pass possible.

Anticipating another great year from Collinsworth, the Hula Bowl invited him to play before the 1980 season began. "That was a big deal for me," Collinsworth said.

But halfway into the season, Collinsworth had only ten catches or so. "I remember they posted the SEC stats on the board and my name was nowhere to be found," Collinsworth said. Disenchanted, Hula Bowl officials sent him a notice that he was no longer invited.

"That really fired me up," Collinsworth said. He went on a tear, making 30 catches in the last five games of the season to lead the SEC in receiving.

The Hula Bowl promptly issued another invitation, but Collinsworth told them to forget it. "The Japan Bowl wanted me, and I'd never been to Japan so I accepted."

That civic club with membership by invitation only. The bleachers where you sit while others frolic in the sky boxes. That neighborhood you can't afford a house in. You know all about being shut out of some club, some group, some place. "Exclusive" is the word that keeps you out.

The Hebrew people, too, knew about being told to keep out; only the priests could come into the presence of the holy and survive. Then along came Jesus to kick that barrier down and give us direct access to God.

In the process, though, Jesus created another exclusive club; its members are his followers, Christians, those who believe he is the Son of God and the savior of the world. This club, though, extends a membership invitation to everyone in the whole wide world; no one is excluded. Whether you're in or out depends on your response to Jesus, not on arbitrary gatekeepers.

There are clubs you can't belong to, neighborhoods you can't live in, schools you can't get into, but the roads are always open.

-- *Nike*

Christianity is an exclusive club, but an invitation is extended to everyone and no one is denied entry.

DAY 33

FLOOR SHOW

Read Luke 15:1-10.

*"There is rejoicing in the presence of the angels of God
over one sinner who repents" (v. 10).*

The Gators celebrated their second consecutive basketball
national championship with video tributes, confetti, trophies,
speeches – and a floor.

After the Gators demolished Ohio State 84-75 on April 2, 2007,
to claim the title, an overflow crowd packed O'Connell Center on
Friday, April 6, to celebrate. The conversation piece of the celebration was the floor of the Georgia Dome in Atlanta on which
the Gators had triumphed. The University Athletic Association
purchased the floor for $71,000 and had it shipped in time for the
ceremony.

But the floor wasn't just there to show off; it was a unique
souvenir of the most glorious period in Florida's basketball
history. The fans of other schools have T-shirts and mugs; Gator
fans have one-by-two-foot chunks of the actual floor on which
the championship was won. After the ceremony, the floor was
cut into 2,200 sections that sold for $199 each with proceeds
benefitting university scholarship funds. A similar project was
undertaken following the 2006 season with the floor of the RCA
Dome in Indianapolis, purchased for $70,000.

"It's great to be a Gator and I'm glad I can share this championship with you all," Coach Billy Donovan told the cheering crowd.

GATORS

The players hit the floor from the stands with senior Chris Richard holding the NCAA Championship trophy, gathering to watch "One Shining Moment," a video tribute to the 2007 NCAA tournament and the national champions. Then blue and orange confetti and unrestrained cheering showered the team as they left that championship floor one last time.

The Florida Gators really know how to celebrate!

Florida just whipped Florida State. You got that new job or that promotion. You just held your newborn child in your arms. Life has those grand moments that call for celebration. You may jump up and down and scream in a wild frenzy at Florida Field or share a quiet, sedate candlelight dinner at home -- but you celebrate.

Consider then a celebration that is beyond our imagining, one that fills every niche and corner of the very home of God and the angels. Imagine a celebration in Heaven, which also has its grand moments.

They are touched off when someone comes to faith in Jesus. Heaven itself rings with the joyous sounds of the singing and dancing of the celebrating angels. Even God rejoices when just one person – you or someone you have introduced to Christ? -- turns to him.

When you said "yes" to Christ, you made the angels dance.

When it comes to celebrating, act like you've been there before.
-- Terry Bowden

God himself joins the angels in heavenly celebration when a single person turns to him through faith in Jesus.

DAY 34

MISSION POSSIBLE

Read Genesis 18:1-15.

"Is anything too hard for the Lord?" (v. 14a)

The college recruiters all told Jimmy Dunn he was too small to play college football even in the 1950s before behemoths roamed the gridiron.

"I would probably have said the same thing," Dunn recalled. "It's one thing to see you on film and then they'd walk in the door and go, 'Dang, you need to be about 25 pounds heavier.' They all recommended I join the service and play there, get a little older and bigger and stronger."

With a little urging from Dunn's high school coach, Florida State offered him a one-year scholarship with the chance to make the team in the spring. But when Dunn put on a show in the high school all-star game in Gainesville, Florida offered him a four-year scholarship on the spot. Dunn accepted, figuring he could get his degree "even though it was unlikely he would be a part of the football team for long."

Dunn did stay with the team, becoming the starting quarterback as a sophomore and playing at 142 pounds, except for the time he got the flu and dropped five pounds. His metabolism consistently defied every scheme the coaching staff could come up with to put some weight on him.

Florida's "Mighty Mite" broke Georgia's heart in 1958 with

GATORS

an electrifying 76-yard fourth-quarter run for a 7-6 win, and he was the MVP of the 21-7 win over FSU that year in the first-ever meeting between the two schools. He quarterbacked the Gators to two top-20 rankings and their second-ever bowl game.

Dunn did quite all right for someone who supposedly was too small.

You've probably never tried a whole bunch of things you've dreamed about doing at one time or another. Like starting your own business. Going back to school. Campaigning for elected office. Running a marathon.

But what holds you back? Perhaps you hesitate because you see only your limitations, both those you've imposed on yourself and those of which others constantly remind you. But maybe as Jimmy Dunn did, it's time you ignored what everybody says. Maybe it's time to see yourself the way God does.

God sees you as you are and also as you can be. In God's eyes, your possibilities are limitless. The realization of those latent possibilities, however, depends upon your depending upon God for direction, guidance, and strength. While you may quail in the face of the challenge that lies before you, nothing is too hard for the Lord.

You can free yourself from that which blights your dreams by depending not on yourself but on God.

First, I prepare. Then I have faith.

-- Joe Namath

When you depend upon God rather than yourself, all missions are possible.

LEVEL PLAYING FIELD

Read Romans 3:21-26.

"There is no distinction, since all have sinned and fall short of the glory of God" (vv. 22b-23 NRSV).

Tennessee didn't cheat in leveling the playing field before the 1928 game with Florida, but the Volunteers may well have stretched the limits of ethical behavior.

Marty Cohen wrote that "for more than 50 years, and maybe forever to long-time Gators, the 1928 team was considered the finest in school history." Using first-year coach Charley Bachman's "Notre Dame formations," the Gators "were a scoring juggernaut." Long before the age of today's wide-open offenses, Florida averaged slightly better than 40 points per game – tops in the country -- in going 8-0. The team had "a fancy-stepping backfield" remembered in Gator lore as the "Phantom Four": quarterback "Cannonball" Clyde Crabtree, who could pass with either hand, Royce Goodbread, Rainey Cawthon, and Carl Brumbaugh. End Dale Van Sickel was Florida's first All-America.

The team entered the season-ending game against Tennessee in Knoxville with everything on the line: a Southern Conference title, the national championship, and a trip to the Rose Bowl. The speedy and nimble Gators were expected to run around and past the slower Volunteers.

Game day dawned bitterly cold, but even worse, the playing field was deep in mud, "perfect conditions to slow down the

GATORS

potent Gators." An irate Bachman accused Tennessee coach Bob Neyland of hosing down the field to create a slow track. Neyland's reply was that an unexpected heavy frost had hit the area and when the ice had melted, the mud was left behind. No one on the Gator side bought his excuse.

The playing field thus leveled, Tennessee pulled off a 13-12 upset.

We should face up to one of life's basic facts: Its playing field isn't level. Others, it seems, get all the breaks. They get the cushy job; they win the lottery; their father owns the business. Some people – perhaps undeservedly -- just have it made.

That said, we just have to accept that the playing field isn't level and get over it. Dwelling on life's inequities can create only bitterness and cynicism, leading us to grumble about what we don't have while ignoring the blessings God continuously showers upon us. A moment's pause and reflection is all it takes for us to call to mind any number of friends, acquaintances, and strangers with whom we would not exchange situations.

The only place in life where we really stand on a level playing field is before God. There, all people are equal because we all need the lifeline God offers through Jesus — and we all have access to it.

That 1928 team, on a dry field, not a team in America could have beaten us.
— Florida head coach Charley Bachman (1928-32)

Unlike life's playing field, God's playing field is level because everyone has equal access to what God has done through Jesus Christ.

REST EASY

Read Hebrews 4:1-11.

"There remains, then, a Sabbath rest for the people of God; for anyone who enters God's rest also rests from his own work, just as God did from his. Let us, therefore, make every effort to enter that rest" (vv. 9-11).

Angie McGinnis needed to get away from Florida volleyball, so she really got away. She went home to Michigan.

McGinnis is one of Florida's greatest volleyball players ever, the best setter in school history. She set almost forty career, season, and match records at Florida and finished her career in 2007 as the school's all-time assists leader with 5,784. She was a three-time All-America and twice was the SEC Player of the Year.

In the summer of 2007 before her senior season, McGinnis figured she needed a rest. She had spent the past four summers training with the USA National Team in Colorado Springs and the last three seasons as the starting setter for the Gators. So she went home to Fraser, Mich., and coached some.

"Her taking a break from volleyball was probably the best thing for her," said teammate Kisya Killingsworth. "She came back a whole new person, a whole new setter." Gators coach Mary Wise agreed: "For Angie just to have some time to have her body recover was important."

The decision was easy for McGinnis. "I'm a big homebody," she said. "Going home gave me a little break from the college atmosphere. When I got back down here, I was ready to train and ready to go."

Renewed and refreshed, she returned to Gainesville the last part of the summer and hit the weights with a passion and a dedication that made her an even better player – which was certainly disconcerting for the rest of the SEC.

All because she took a break.

As part of the natural rhythm of life, rest is important to maintain physical health. Rest has different images, though: a good eight hours in the sack; a Saturday morning that begins in the backyard with the paper and a pot of coffee; a vacation in the mountains where the most strenuous thing you do is change position in the hot tub.

Rest is also part of the rhythm and the health of your spiritual life. Often we envision the faithful person as always busy, always doing something for God whether it's teaching Sunday school or showing up at church every time the doors open.

But God himself rested from work, and in blessing us with the Sabbath, he calls us into a time of rest. To rest by simply spending time in the presence of God is to receive spiritual revitalization and rejuvenation. Sleep refreshes your body and your mind; God's rest refreshes your soul.

You have peace of mind and can enjoy yourself, get more sleep, and rest when you know that it was a one hundred percent effort that you gave – win or lose.

-- NHL legend Gordie Howe

God promises you a spiritual rest that renews and refreshes your soul.

DAY 37

PAYBACK

Read Matthew 5: 38-42.

"I tell you, Do not resist an evil person. If someone strikes you on the right cheek, turn to him the other also" (v. 39).

The Gators didn't forget it, Georgia's infamous and insulting celebration in 2007. For a year they waited for revenge. And, oh, how they got it.

The Bulldogs got what was due them on Nov. 1, 2008. But that was simply the climactic moment the Gators had been building up to for some time.

Revenge was on the mind of strength and conditioning coach Mickey Marotti in his off-season workouts. He required players to do 42 reps at each station. The number was not coincidental; it was the number of points Georgia scored in the 2007 game. Marotti also added sets of 188 push-ups, sit-ups, and crunches, so the Gators would remember the 188 yards Knowshon Moreno gained on them. Then after the work-outs, when the players "dragged themselves back to their lockers, ready to puke," they were greeted by pictures of the Georgia players flooding the field after 2007's first touchdown.

So payback was on the Gators' minds from the first play of the 2008 game – so much so that the Dogs were never really in the game. Florida led 14-3 at halftime, and cornerback Joe Haden cinched the deal when he returned an interception 88 yards to the Georgia one in the third quarter. Tim Tebow accounted for five touchdowns and broke Emmitt Smith's school record for rushing touchdowns. The Gators blasted Georgia 49-10, the second-most lopsided Florida win in the series.

The victorious Gators then stood in the center of the field, helmets in the air, and sang the fight song as the band played. Payback achieved.

The very nature of an intense rivalry such as Florida-Georgia is that the loser will seek payback for the defeat of the season before. But what about in life when somebody's done you wrong; is it time to get even?

The problem with revenge in real-life is that it isn't as clear-cut as a scoreboard. Life is so messy that any attempt at revenge is often inadequate or, worse, backfires and injures you.

As a result, you remain gripped by resentment and anger, which hurts you and no one else. You poison your own happiness while that other person goes blithely about her business. The only way someone who has hurt you can keep hurting you is if you're a willing participant.

But it doesn't have to be that way. Jesus ushered in a new way of living when he taught that we are not to seek revenge for personal wrongs and injuries. Let it go and go on with your life. What a relief!

That wasn't right. It was a bad deal. And it will forever be in the mind of Urban Meyer and in the mind of our football team.
-- Urban Meyer on Georgia's touchdown celebration in 2007

Resentment and anger over a wrong injures you,
not the other person, so forget it
-- just as Jesus taught.

DAY 38

GATOR BAIT

Read Psalm 139:1-18.

"For you created my inmost being; you knit me together in my mother's womb. I praise you because I am fearfully and wonderfully made" (vv. 13-14).

Bulldogs and Tigers and the like -- they're as common as Florida touchdowns. But only one team has the Gators.

While many schools floundered in the early days in their search for a suitably fearsome symbol, Florida's uniquely appropriate mascot was born in 1907, only the second season of Florida football. The story goes that in the fall of 1907, Phillip Miller, owner-operator of a drug and stationery store in Gainesville that was a popular student hangout, visited his son, Austin, at the University of Virginia. He saw some collegiate pennants and banners there and thought they would sell well in his store.

So Miller contacted the outfit that made them but found himself flummoxed when company reps showed him pennants from Yale and Princeton with Tigers and Bulldogs and then asked him for a Florida emblem to put on his pennants. He realized Florida had none, so on the spur of the moment, he replied, "Alligators" because they were native to Florida and no other school had that nickname. Austin went to the University of Virginia library, found a photo of an alligator, and traced it.

By the fall of 1908, in time for football season, a six-foot-by-three-foot blue banner with an orange alligator was the centerpiece of Miller's store, and sales of the collegiate items took off. Soon Miller had to order all sorts of pennants and banners with the "Florida Alligator" on them.

For many years, Florida's teams were the "Alligators," and some pompous sportswriters sometimes referred to the "Saurians," a fancy Greek word for a group of reptiles. Today, though, they're the "Gators" and nothing else.

Animals such as full-grown alligators elicit our awe and our respect. Nothing enlivens a trip more than glimpsing turkeys, bears, or deer in the wild. Admit it: You go along with the kids' trip to the zoo because you think it's a cool place too. All that variety of life is mind-boggling. Who could conceive of an alligator, a walrus, a moose, or a prairie dog? Who could possibly have that rich an imagination?

But the next time you're in a crowd, look around at the parade of faces. Who could come up with the idea for all those different people? For that matter, who could conceive of you? You are unique, a masterpiece who will never be duplicated.

The master creator, God Almighty, is behind it all. He thought of you and brought you into being. If you had a manufacturer's label, it might say, "Lovingly, fearfully, and wonderfully handmade in Heaven by #1 -- God."

I had no idea it would stick or even be popular with the student body.
-- Austin Miller on the Alligator nickname

Alligators are certainly among God's most awesome creations, but the real masterpiece is you.

FOUND WANTING

Read Psalm 73:23-28.

*"Whom have I in heaven but you? And earth has nothing
I desire besides you" (v. 25).*

He wasn't that big. He wasn't that fast. He didn't look much like
a running back. He was just the best there's ever been.

Nobody really ever knew what to make of Emmitt Smith. One
scout pegged him as a bust coming out of high school, "just a
lugger." Another said he was the best high-school player in the
country.

In his second game in Gainesville in 1987, he let everybody
know what he really was about. He hit a hole in the second
quarter against Tulsa, made one cut, and ripped off a 66-yard
touchdown. Emmitt had arrived. "We needed something to spark
us," quarterback Kerwin Bell said, "and that run did it." Yes, it
did. Florida won 52-0 in what became known in Gator lore as
"Emmitt's coming out party."

Before he left Gainesville after his junior season, Emmitt set 58
Florida records. He was the SEC Player of the Year and a unani-
mous All-America in 1989. Sixteen professional teams made the
same mistake that so-called recruiting expert had made back in
high school: They passed on Emmitt. The Dallas Cowboys drafted
him seventeenth, and he became the NFL's all-time leading rusher.
He is a member of both the college and the pro halls of fame.

And through it all, Emmitt was still too slow and too small.

How in the world did he do it? He once provided the answer. "If you want to get through a hole bad enough, you'll get through it," he said. Emmitt wanted it.

What do you want out of life? A loving, caring family, a home of your own, the respect of those whom you admire? Our heart's desires can elevate us to greatness and goodness, but they can also plunge us into destruction, despair, and evil. Drugs, alcohol, control, sex, power, worldly success: Do these desires motivate you?

Desires are not inherently evil or bad for you; after all, God planted the capacity to desire in us. The key is determining which of your heart's desires are healthful and are worth pursuing and which are dangerous and are best avoided.

Not surprisingly, the answer to the dilemma lies with God. You consult the one whose own heart's desire is for what is unequivocally best for you, who is driven only by his unqualified love for you. You match what you want for yourself with what God wants for you.

Your deepest heart's desire must be the establishment and maintenance of an intimate relationship with God.

In football, you get on that field and become what you want to become. If you're ever going to do well, you have to put heart and soul in it.
— Gator halfback Larry Dupree (1962-64)

Whether our desires drive us to greatness or to destruction is determined by whether they are also God's desires for our lives.

DAY 40

FATHER FIGURE

Read Matthew 3:13-17.

"A voice from heaven said, 'This is my Son, whom I love; with him I am well pleased'" (v. 17).

They were the fabulous four who led Florida to two straight NCAA championships in 2006 and 2007: Al Horford, Joakim Noah, Corey Brewer, and Taurean Green. Three of them had fathers who were professional athletes. The fourth was "a peon compared to those guys," according to his wife. But he inspired his son nevertheless.

Horford's dad was a first-round NBA draft-pick; Green's father once scored 1,000 points in an NBA season; Noah's old man won the French Open. And Brewer's father, Ellis? He raised tobacco and soybeans in Tennessee until heart troubles made that impossible. "I ain't done nothing," he said, "but grow up on a farm."

Ellis Brewer wanted more for his boy than the hardscrabble life on the farm. "I tried to tell him he can't grow up like I did," Dad said. "I told him he had to get a good education. . . . You don't want to raise tobacco for a living." The senior Brewer delivered his message with more than words. By the time Corey was 5, he was in the hot sun stripping tobacco; he started driving a tractor when he was 8. "Working in the field, man, that was a great lesson," he said.

The son learned the lesson so well tobacco farming is not a part of his present or his future. As Corey once said, "My daddy's not famous, but he's worked hard all his life." And inspired his son to become a Gator legend, a national champion, and a professional basketball player. All of which, Pat Dooley wrote, "makes him famous enough."

American society largely belittles and marginalizes fathers and their influence upon their sons. Men are perceived as necessary to effect pregnancy; after that, they can leave and everybody's better off.

But we need look in only two places to appreciate the enormity of that misconception: our jails – packed with males who lacked the influence of fathers in their lives as they grew up -- and the Bible. God – being God – could have chosen any relationship he desired between Jesus and himself, including society's approach of irrelevancy. Instead, the most important relationship in all of history was that of father-son.

God obviously believes a close, loving relationship between fathers and sons, like that of Corey and Ellis Brewer, is crucial. For men and women to espouse otherwise or for men to walk blithely and carelessly out of their children's lives constitutes disobedience to the divine will.

Simply put, God loves fathers. After all, he is one.

My dad was a huge influence on me. I imagine if he had put a wrench in my hand I would have been a great mechanic.
-- Pete Maravich

**Fatherhood is a tough job, but a model
for the father-child relationship is found
in that of Jesus the Son with God the Father.**

EXCUSES, EXCUSES

Read Luke 9:57-62.

"Another said, 'I will follow you, Lord; but first let me go back and say good-by to my family'" (v. 61).

The Florida-Georgia series was the perfect example of what Steve Spurrier meant when he declared that Florida Gators -- players and fans alike -- shouldn't make any excuses.

As Peter Kerasotis noted in *Stadium Stories: Florida Gators*, when Spurrier arrived in Gainesville, rumblings abounded about moving the Florida-Georgia game out of Jacksonville. The widespread perception was that for whatever reasons the Gators couldn't consistently whip Georgia there, so the series should be moved to home-and home.

Spurrier would have none of that; he felt the advantage of playing the game in Jacksonville belonged exclusively to the Gators.

"Not only does Georgia have to come to the state of Florida every year to play the game," he said, "but they have to play in a stadium called the Gator Bowl. They also have to take a bus to Atlanta and then fly to Jacksonville. All we have to do is bus over to Jacksonville."

So with no excuses in tow, the Gators went out and claimed Jacksonville as their own. During the Spurrier years, Florida went 11-1 against Georgia, and often the Gators won big. The domination continued under both Ron Zook and Urban Meyer.

GATORS

Before Spurrier left, the Bulldogs and their fans were the ones who were grumbling about packing their bags and moving the game out of Jacksonville. Not that it would have made any difference since two of the wins of the Spurrier era were home-and-home because of renovations of the Gator Bowl.

Georgia fans became the ones making excuses for not winning. And that hasn't changed.

Has some of your most creative thinking involved reasons for not going in to work? Have you discovered that an unintended benefit of computers is that you can always blame them for the destruction of all your hard work? Don't you manage to stammer or stutter some justification when a state trooper pulls you over? We're usually pretty good at making excuses to cover our failures or to get out of something we don't particularly want to do.

That holds true for our faith life also. The Bible is too hard to understand so I won't read it; the weather's too pretty to be shut up in church; praying in public is embarrassing and I'm not very good at it anyway. The plain truth is, though, that whatever excuses we make for not following Jesus wholeheartedly are not good enough.

Jesus made no excuses to avoid dying for us; we should offer none to avoid living for him.

There are a thousand reasons for failure but not a single excuse.
-- Former NFL player Mike Reid

**Try though we might, no excuses can justify
our failure to follow Jesus.**

DAY 42

FACING THE MUSIC

Read Psalm 98.

"Sing to the Lord a new song, for he has done marvelous things" (v. 1).

If it's game day at The Swamp, then frenzied, exuberant, and loud music fills the air. The most enthusiastic music makers of them all sit together and dress alike. They're the University of Florida Fightin' Gator Marching Band.

Football at Florida officially begin in 1906, but not until 1914 did Pug Hamilton organize a school band. It had only sixteen members and was called the Cadet Band.

The first offices were in Anderson Hall, and the first band room was in the women's gymnasium. The first paid band director, R. Dewitt Brown, arrived in 1920. The first female member of the band was Sophy Mae Mitchell, who blazed a trail in 1948. She carried the band's banner her first year and was invited to play the bell lyre for the rest of her college career.

Also known as "The Pride of the Sunshine," the Fightin' Gator Marching Band is part of some of the greatest traditions in all of college football. The block "F," the spelling out of "Gators," and the forming of the tunnel through which the football players take the field are all part of the pregame ritual that whips the Gator faithful into an orange and blue lather.

Perhaps the band's best-known tradition is the playing of "We Are the Boys" at the end of the third quarter. The band begins with a short introduction and then sets the whole crowd into a swaying motion in one of the most stirring moments in college football.

A new tradition was begun by Coach Urban Meyer in 2005, who after a game leads the team over to the band where everyone sings the "Alma Mater" and the fight song and Meyer shakes the band director's hand.

When the Gator Marching Band shows up, music fills the air.

Maybe you can't play a lick or carry a tune in the proverbial bucket. Or perhaps you do know your way around a guitar or a keyboard and can sing "We Are the Boys" on karaoke night without closing the joint down.

Unless you're a professional musician, however, how well you play or sing really doesn't matter. What counts is that you have music in your heart and sometimes you have to turn it loose.

Worshipping God has always included music in some form. That same boisterous and musical enthusiasm you exhibit at the end of the third quarter of the Gator games should be a part of the joy you have in your personal worship of God.

When you consider that God loves you, he always will, and he has arranged through Jesus for you to spend eternity with him, how can that song God put in your heart not burst forth?

I like it because it plays old music.
                    -- Pitcher Tug McGraw on his '54 Buick

You call it music; others may call it noise;
God calls it praise.

DAY 43

UNEXPECTEDLY

Read Luke 2:1-20.

*"She gave birth to her firstborn, a son. She wrapped him
in cloths and placed him in a manger, because there was
no room for them in the inn" (v. 7).*

As the tenth-ranked Gators of 1997 prepared for the season-
ending game against second-ranked and undefeated FSU, the
quarterback situation was a mess. Florida fans debated who
would lead the team against the Seminoles: Doug Johnson, Noah
Brindise, or Jesse Palmer. They never expected what they got.

The Tuesday before the game coach Steve Spurrier surprised
everyone by announcing that Johnson and Brindise would alternate – on every play. "It was a shock to the whole team," Johnson
said. "When he told us we were going to alternate on every play,
we looked at each other like, 'What is he talking about?'" Brindise
said. "It was a weird feeling all week."

Spurrier was true to his word. On the first play, Brindise
completed a pass and immediately ran to the sidelines. Johnson
ran a play and then Brindise went back in. Brindise said, "My dad
knew about it, but an uncle of mine started booing." Unorthodox
use of quarterbacks or not, the game was one of the greatest ever
at Florida Field. The Gators won 32-29 on a late Fred Taylor touchdown set up by a Johnson completion to Jacquez Green.

After Duane Thomas wrapped up the upset win by nabbing
an interception following the touchdown, Johnson went in for

the first play, and senior Brindise told Spurrier, "I'm taking the last snap." He did, finishing off an unexpected win that featured unexpected handling of the quarterbacks. (Perhaps equally unexpected was the way Spurrier used his quarterbacks in the 21-6 win over Penn State in the Citrus Bowl: He alternated all three of them.)

Just like Steve Spurrier's surprise against FSU, we think we've got everything figured out and planned for, and then something unexpected happens. Someone gets ill; you fall in love; you lose your job; you're going to have another child. Life surprises us with its bizarre twists and turns.

God is that way too, catching us unawares to remind us he's still around. A friend who hears you're down and stops by, a child's laugh, an achingly beautiful sunset -- unexpected moments of love and beauty. God is like that, always doing something in our lives we didn't expect.

But why shouldn't he? There is nothing God can't do. The only factor limiting what God can do is the paucity of our own faith.

Expect the unexpected from God, this same deity who unexpectedly came to live among us as a man. He does, by the way, expect a response from you.

Willie Jackson, Jr. was probably the most talented receiver I ever played with at Florida. He was a freshman walk-on who came out of nowhere.
– Shane Matthews

God does the unexpected to remind you
of his presence -- like showing up as Jesus
– and now he expects a response from you.

DAY 44

ONE TOUGH COOKIE

Read 2 Corinthians 11:21-29.

"Besides everything else, I face daily the pressure of my concern for all the churches" (v. 28).

Danny Wuerffel may have clinched the Heisman Trophy in the only game the Gators lost in the 1996 national championship season. In that bitter loss to Florida State, he demonstrated not exceptional passing skills but exceptional toughness and courage.

A pair of undefeateds -- number one and number two – met that incredible November day in Tallahassee with the Seminoles coming away with a 24-21 win. After the game, Steve Spurrier expressed his conviction that FSU had gone headhunting and had intentionally tried to knock his quarterback out of the game. "When you watch the replays, these guys aren't just shoving Danny down," Spurrier fulminated. "They're loading up. They're hitting him under the jaw with their helmets. They're spearing him. They're burying him." Spurrier even compiled a tape of all the vicious late hits and sent it to the SEC office.

Gator trainers said after the game "Wuerffel looked like he'd been beaten up." He "was so battered he couldn't even muster the strength to hug his mother." Thirty-five times that afternoon Danny Wuerffel went down -- and thirty-five times Danny Wuerffel got back up. That game changed the perception many Heisman voters had of Wuerffel as they realized for the first time just how tough he was and that playing in Spurrier's system required a special quarterback. They understood that Danny Wuerffel was one tough cookie.

In the rematch in the Sugar Bowl, he reminded everyone just how special he was. Wuerffel was 18 of 34 passing for 308 yards and three touchdowns in the 52-20 romp over the Seminoles.

You don't have to be a legendary Gator quarterback to be tough. In America today, toughness isn't restricted to brute strength and physical accomplishments. Going to work every morning even when you're ill, sticking by your rules for your children in a society that ridicules parental authority, making hard decisions about your aging parents' care often over their objections — you've got to be tough every day just to live honorably, decently, and justly.

Living faithfully requires toughness, too, though in America chances are you won't be imprisoned, stoned, or flogged this week for your faith as Paul was. Still, contemporary society exerts subtle, psychological, daily pressures on you to turn your back on your faith and your values. Popular culture promotes atheism, promiscuity, and gutter language; your children's schools have kicked God out; the corporate culture advocates amorality before the shrine of the almighty dollar.

You have to hang tough to keep the faith.

Winning isn't imperative, but getting tougher in the fourth quarter is.
— Bear Bryant

Life demands more than mere physical toughness;
you must be spiritually tough too.

DAY 45

HOMEBODY

Read 2 Corinthians 5:1-10.

"We . . . would prefer to be away from the body and at home with the Lord" (v. 8).

The college scouts lost track of Lonnika Thompson.

In August 2005, Hurricane Katrina interrupted Thompson's routine odyssey to college basketball. Her family fled New Orleans and Lonnika landed with relatives in Jonesboro, Ga. Nobody in her family foresaw the extent of the disaster about to strike. "I just thought we'd have a lot of rain and wind and we'd be back home in three days," Thompson said.

The storm flooded the Thompson home and forced Lonnika to start her senior year in Georgia. Not until January 2006 did her high school reopen, allowing her to return to New Orleans though she lived with a friend because her house was in ruins.

Even though her father had notified them of where Lonnika was, the colleges recruiting her seemed to lose interest. She landed at Trinity Valley Community College in Texas where she eventually got a phone call that floored her; new Gators head coach Amanda Butler needed a point guard and had determined that Thompson was the best one available. "I couldn't believe it was her calling," Thompson said.

So she moved again, this time finding a new home in Gainesville and starting right away as a sophomore in the 2007-08 season.

And her home in New Orleans? Despite the extensive water damage, the infrastructure was sound. By November 2007, the house was rebuilt, one of the first. "It was basically the same but brand new," Thompson said. "It's home."

Ultimately, Lonnika Thompson wound up with two homes: one with her Gainesville family and one with her New Orleans family.

Home is not necessarily a matter of geography. It may be that place you share with your spouse and your children, whether it's Florida or Louisiana. You may feel at home when you return to Gainesville, wondering why you were so eager to leave in the first place. Maybe the home you grew up in still feels like an old shoe, a little worn but comfortable and inviting.

God planted that sense of home in us because he is a God of place, and our place is with him. Thus, we may live a few blocks away from our parents and grandparents or we may relocate every few years, but we still will sometimes feel as though we don't really belong no matter where we are.

We don't; our true home is with God in the place Jesus has gone ahead to prepare for us. We are homebodies and we are perpetually homesick.

Former players should know that, no matter what, they always have a home here.

– Steve Spurrier

We are continually homesick for our real home, which is with God in Heaven.

DAY 46

RAIN CHECK

Read Genesis 9:8-17.

*"I establish my covenant with you: Never again will all
life be cut off by the waters of a flood; never again will
there be a flood to destroy the earth" (v. 11).*

What was it that would entice a highly recruited player who
would become one of Florida's greatest receivers ever to come to
Gainesville? The beautiful girls? The university's academic excellence? The acumen of the coaching staff or a personal relationship
with one of the coaches?

None of these things cinched it for Charlie Casey. Rather, he
made his mind up when he landed in Florida on a recruiting trip
during the winter -- and it wasn't raining.

Casey was an All-American end in 1965 and All-SEC in 1964
and 1965. Though he played long before the age of wide-open
offenses, his name is still consistently found in the Florida record
book.

From Atlanta, Casey began to draw the attention of college
recruiters even though he wasn't particularly fast and had small
hands. But, as Casey said, "I could do one thing – catch the ball.
. . . I guess it was just hand-eye coordination from playing baseball for so many years." His first choice was Georgia Tech, and a
recruiting trip during which he met legendary coach Bobby Dodd
seemed to close the deal. But Casey also took trips to Clemson,
South Carolina, Georgia, Florida State – and Florida.

That fated trip to Gainesville changed his mind. When he boarded the plane in Atlanta for Jacksonville during his senior basketball season, sleeting rain pelted the passengers. When he landed in Jacksonville, "It was 72 and beautiful," Casey said. "I was thinking, 'Why would anyone want to leave here?' That sold me."

The Gators landed an All-American end – because it wasn't raining.

The kids are on go for their picnic. Your golf game is set. You have rib eyes and smoked sausage ready for the grill when the gang comes over tonight. And then it rains.

Sometimes you can slog on if the rain doesn't get too heavy. Often, however, the rain simply washes away your carefully laid plans, and you can't do anything about it.

Rain falls when and where it wants to without checking with you. It answers only to God, the one who controls the heavens from which it comes, the ground on which it falls, and everything in between -- territory that should include you.

Though God has absolute dominance over the rain, he will take control of your life only if you let him. In daily seeking his will for your life, you discover that you can live so as to be walking in the sunshine even when it's raining.

Don't pray when it rains if you don't pray when the sun shines.
-- Pitcher and philosopher Leroy "Satchel" Paige

Into each life some rain must fall, but you can live in the glorious light of God's love even during a downpour.

DAY 47

JUST PERFECT

Read Matthew 5:43-48.

"Be perfect, therefore, as your heavenly Father is perfect"
(v. 48).

Melanie Sinclair was perfect. Not once but twice.

Sinclair was a redshirt freshman on March 2, 2007, when she became the first Florida gymnast in history to nail more than one perfect 10.0 on bars in a career. Her perfect score was crucial to the top-ranked Gators' win over 22nd-ranked North Carolina State.

"Wow! Did I just do that again? Are you serious?" Sinclair said she thought when she stuck a flawless landing off a double layout and flashed a radiant smile toward the O'Connell Center ceiling. The crowd of more than 5,000 knew what they had seen; they erupted immediately into wild cheers. When the judges flashed the perfect score, the crowd saluted Sinclair with a standing ovation.

"She's capable of a 10 every time she's up there," her coach, Rhonda Faehn, said. "She's so clean and has the highest degree of difficulty. All she needs is to stick that landing, and she did that tonight."

Sinclair also stuck it just two weeks earlier, on Feb. 16, in the Gators' win over Kentucky when she recorded her first 10. That performance propelled her into some elite company; only three other Florida gymnasts had ever recorded a perfect score on bars: Erin Pendleton in 2003, Kristen Guise in 1996, and Amy Myerson in 1996. Guise, who was part of the crowd the night Sinclair got her second 10, remarked upon the difficulty of getting two 10s, but then added, "When you're as good as these girls are it looks easy."

It wasn't easy for Melanie Sinclair, but it was perfect.

Nobody's perfect; we all make mistakes every day. We botch our personal relationships; at work we seek competence, not perfection. To insist upon personal or professional perfection in our lives is to establish an impossibly high standard that eventually destroys us physically, emotionally, and mentally.

Yet that is exactly the standard God sets for us. Our love is to be perfect, never ceasing, never failing, never qualified – just the way God loves us. And Jesus didn't limit his command to only preachers and goody-two-shoes types. All of his disciples are to be perfect as they navigate their way through the world's ambiguous definition and understanding of love.

But that's impossible! Well, not necessarily if to love perfectly is to serve God wholeheartedly and to follow Jesus with single-minded devotion. Anyhow, in his perfect love for us, God makes allowance for our imperfect love and the consequences of it in the perfection of Jesus.

Practice does not make you perfect as nobody is perfect, but it does make you better.
--Soccer coach Adrian Parrish

In his perfect love for us, God provides a way
for us to escape the consequences
of our imperfect love for him: Jesus.

DAY 48

HOME-FIELD ADVANTAGE

Read Joshua 24:14-27.

"Choose for yourselves this day whom you will serve. . . .
But as for me and my household, we will serve the Lord"
(v. 15).

It's an incredible advantage."

Thus spoke Peyton Manning about playing in The Swamp, and he wasn't talking about Tennessee getting any help. The Swamp may well provide Florida with the greatest home-field advantage in college football.

The numbers don't lie: You don't come sashaying into Gainesville and win very often. From 1990 when Steve Spurrier arrived through the 2008 season, the Gators were an incredible 106-13 in The Swamp, the second-best winning percentage in college football during that stretch.

The Swamp's reputation is widespread. Matthew Waxman of *Sports Illustrated* said it's been called "'the loudest, most obnoxious and notorious piece of real estate' in college football. The students do the chomp in prime seats between the 25- and 50-yard lines. To every non-Gator lover who has set foot in the Swamp, admit it: The thought I might die tonight has crossed your mind."

Part of the advantage lies in the way Florida Field was constructed. As Waxman noted, "Both sides of the stadium rise almost vertically, keeping the noise in and the fans on top of the action."

But the Gators won at home even before Florida Field existed. Prior to 1930, Florida played its home games at Fleming Field, which was located just north of the current stadium. Fans watched the games from the hoods of their parked cars along the sidelines. And what they mostly watched was a winner: From 1908 through 1915, the Gators were undefeated at home with an incredible 25-0-1 record.

When the Gators play at home, they have the advantage.

You enter your home to find love, security, and joy. It's the place where your heart feels warmest, your laughter comes easiest, and your life is its richest. It is the center of and the reason for everything you do and everything you are.

How can a home be such a place?

If it is a home where grace is spoken before every meal, it is such a place. If it is a home where the Bible is read, studied, and discussed by the whole family gathered together, it is such a place. If it is a home that serves as a jumping-off point for the whole family to go to church, not just on Sunday morning and not just occasionally, but regularly, it is such a place. If it is a home where the name of God is spoken with reverence and awe and not with disrespect and indifference, it is such a place.

In other words, a house becomes a true home when God is part of the family.

Sure, the home field is an advantage, but so is having a lot of talent.
-- Dan Marino

A home is full when all the family members –
including God -- are present.

DAY 49

IN THE KNOW

Read John 4:19-26, 39-42.

"They said to the woman, . . . 'Now we have heard for ourselves, and we know that this man really is the Savior of the world'" (v. 42).

Ole Miss was going to try a fake punt -- and the Gators knew it.

Florida led only 30-24 in the 2007 game in Oxford with a little more than three minutes left to play. The Rebels faced fourth and eleven at their own 33. Playing the percentages meant punting the ball and hoping your defense could stop the Gators.

Ole Miss hadn't been able to stop Florida all day though, so in effect the Rebs were down to their last chance -- and coach Urban Meyer knew it. "I know that coach [Ed Orgeron]," he said, "and I knew he wasn't going to punt. He was going to try and go win the game."

When the Rebs broke the huddle, they lined up in a "funky punt formation with the entire offensive line to the right of the center." Meyer quickly called a time out to come up with a defense for the fake punt he knew was coming.

Thanks to television and a lengthy commercial break, the time out stretched to two minutes, which gave Meyer plenty of time. "I want to thank CBS, whoever did the game for that time out," Meyer said.

After the time out, the Gators were ready. The Ole Miss punter rolled to his right as though to let fly with a rugby-style punt, then suddenly pulled up, and threw a pass. He completed it to his tight end, but defensive end Jermaine Cunningham was there to make the tackle three yards short of the first down. Game over.

The play "was geared to be a fake punt or go ahead and punt it if we didn't have the numbers on that side of the ball," Orgeron said. "We had the numbers. We just didn't make the play."

Because the Gators knew it was coming.

They just knew in the same way you know certain things in your life. That your spouse loves you, for instance. That you are good at your job. That tea should be iced and sweetened. That a bad day fishing is still better than a good day at work. That the best barbecue comes from a pig. You know these things even though no mathematician or philosopher can prove any of this on paper.

It's the same way with faith in Jesus: You just know that he is God's son and the savior of the world. You know it in the same way that you know the Florida Gators are the only team worth pulling for: with every fiber of your being, with all your heart, your mind, and your soul.

You just know, and because you know him, Jesus knows you. And that is all you really need to know.

You know you're getting old when you start watching golf on TV and enjoying it.

-- *Comedian Larry Miller*

A life of faith is lived in certainty and conviction:
You just know you know.

DAY 50

RIGHT-MINDED

Read Galatians 6:7-10.

"Let us not grow weary in doing what is right, for we will reap at harvest time, if we do not give up" (v. 9 NRSV).

An official's refusal to do the right thing cost Steve Spurrier and the Gators a chance for a last-gap comeback in his last regular-season game.

In 1966, Florida hosted Miami four days after Spurrier was presented the Heisman Trophy. The Gators went into the game favored with an 8-1 record, but Spurrier admitted that they didn't play very well.

Still, they trailed only 21-16 late in the game when they got the ball. Spurrier completed one pass for a first down, and Larry Smith ran a draw to midfield but fumbled.

As Spurrier remembered it, "We were at midfield with lots of time left, and the Miami defensive guy fell on the ball, but it squirted out. Our receiver, Paul Ewaldsen, fell on it. He was on the ground with the ball under his chest. But the referee, instead of waiting to see who had it, came running in and signaled Miami the ball."

The ref refused to change his decision even though Ewaldsen was standing right in front of him holding the ball. Spurrier came running up and confronted the official. "Wait a minute now, our guy has the ball. How can you do that?" Spurrier shouted. The ref answered, "I've already made the call." "That's terrible," Spurrier retorted.

The official was more concerned with the possibility that he might be embarrassed by having to change his call than he was with doing the right thing. The incorrect call stood and Spurrier never got this one last chance to lead yet another Gator comeback.

Doing the right thing is easy when it's little stuff. Giving the quarter back when the cashier gives you too much change, helping a lost child at the mall, or putting a few bucks in the honor box at your favorite fishing hole.

But what about when it costs you? Every day you have multiple chances to do the right thing; in every instance, you have a choice: right or wrong. The factors that weigh into your decisions – including the personal cost to you – reveal much about your character.

Does your doing the right thing ever depend upon your calculation of the odds of getting caught? In the world's eyes, you can't go wrong doing wrong when you won't get caught. That passes for the world's slippery, situational ethics, but it doesn't pass muster with God.

In God's eyes, you can't go wrong doing right. Ever.

When you are doing all the right things, eventually your time is going to come.

– Chris Leak

As far as God is concerned, you can never go wrong doing right.

DAY 51

FAILED EXPECTATIONS

Read John 1:43-51.

"'Nazareth! Can anything good come from there?'
Nathanael asked" (v. 46).

The basketball Gators of 2007 – the defending national champions and the heavy favorites to repeat – were in trouble.

After leading Florida to the national championship in 2006, rather than turning pro, forwards Corey Brewer and Al Horford, center Joakim Noah, and point guard Taurean Green stayed in school. The decision by the four stars to return in itself burdened the team with championship expectations. Nothing but another national title would make the season successful.

In late February, though, a title appeared to be slipping away. The Gators lost three of four games, all by double digits, and looked like anything but conference champions, let alone national champions.

But they got help from an unexpected source who pinpointed the problem. Green's father, Sidney – a former NBA player – took a day off work in Orlando and drove to Gainesville.

Over dinner that night, Green laid it on the line for the four players. "You guys are 25-5, and you're acting like it's the end of the world," he said. And what was the problem? "You're trying to live up to everyone else's expectations, and you're pressing, and it shows." The players nodded their heads in agreement. "You're right," Noah said. "I'm not having any fun."

Green popped into the DVD a copy of their win over Syracuse from the season before. There they were, "running with abandon and playing with the effervescent joy of an unranked team." In their suite that night, they recaptured the "sense of youthful wonder" they had lost beneath the weight of all the expectations.

The Gators didn't lose another game.

The blind date your friend promised would look like Brad Pitt or Jennifer Aniston but resembled a Munster. Your vacation that went downhill after the lost luggage. Often your expectations are raised only to be dashed. Sometimes it's best not to get your hopes up; then at least you have the possibility of being surprised.

Worst of all, perhaps, is when you realize that you are the one not meeting others' expectations. The fact is, though, that you aren't here to live up to what others think of you. Jesus didn't; in part, that's why they killed him. But he did meet God's expectations for his life, which was all that really mattered.

Because God's kingdom is so awesomely majestic, God does have great expectations for any who would enter, and you should not take them lightly. What the world expects from you is of no importance; what God expects from you is paramount.

Other people may not have had high expectations for me, but I had high expectations for myself.

-- Gymnast Shannon Miller

You have little if anything to gain from meeting the world's expectations of you; you have all of eternity to gain from meeting God's.

DAY 52

GOING OUT IN STYLE

Read Matthew 25:14-30.

"Well done, good and faithful servant! . . . Come and share your master's happiness!" (v. 21)

Being asked to resign by the university president was not the way Bob Woodruff wanted to end his career as Florida's head football coach and athletic director, but Woodruff went out with style and class by doing a remarkable thing.

Woodruff arrived in Gainesville in January 1950 with orders to move Florida football into the "modern era" and into the upper echelons of the SEC. He led the Gators to their first-ever bowl game after the 1952 season, a 14-13 Gator-Bowl win over Tulsa, and to the Gator Bowl again in 1958. His overall record was 53-42-6, which at the time made him Florida's winningest coach ever. He championed an expansion of Florida Field that doubled its capacity.

But as Marty Cohen put it, Woodruff's "slow-talking, somewhat gruff demeanor coupled with a conservative, defense-oriented style of football, never grabbed the fancy of Florida followers." By the middle of the 1950s, "rumors of his dismissal pervaded nearly every fall, even though he only suffered two losing seasons and the overall athletic program was in superior health."

Finally, on Dec. 2, 1959, despite a season that ended with the Gators whipping both FSU and Miami and being ranked 18th, UF President J. Wayne Reitz asked for Woodruff's resignation and he turned it in. Instead of just walking away as he could have, though, he stayed on until a new head coach was hired, recruiting 26 players whom he would never coach. Woodruff would later say he was "disappointed and deeply shocked" that his efforts were not more appreciated. Nevertheless, he remained loyal to Florida to the end.

Bob Woodruff chose to go out with style and grace.

You probably have known times in your life when you felt it was necessary to move on. The job at which you had done all you could. The friendship that wasn't close any more. That tearful handing of your daughter to your new son-in-law. Sometimes you have no choice about the change, but you can always choose whether you exit with style and grace, as Bob Woodruff did.

That holds true for life's end. We often picture "going out in style" to mean a fancy funeral with a long black hearse, a huge crowd, lots of flowers, and some famous preachers. At that point, though, you have long since departed this earthly existence. That expensive send-off is for those you left behind.

When it comes to life and death, going out in style means only one thing: leaving with God's praise reverberating through your heavenly-bound soul: "Well done, good and faithful servant."

Don't go to your grave with a life unused.

-- Bobby Bowden

**The only meaningful way to go out in style
is to leave this life with praise from God.**

DAY 53

HOME IMPROVEMENT

Read Ephesians 4:7-16.

*"[The body of Christ may be built up] until we all reach
unity in the faith and in the knowledge of the Son of God
and become mature, attaining to the whole measure of the
fullness of Christ" (v. 13).*

Charley Pell's legacy will probably always be debated by Gator
fans, but as Peter Kerasotis wrote, the Pell years "laid the groundwork for all the bright and wonderful things" that are Florida
football today.

Pell was Florida's head football coach from 1979 until he was
fired three games into the 1984 season. He was 33-26-3 during
his tenure, but the numbers reveal little. He was obsessed with
winning, declaring on NBC's *Dateline* in 1995, 'There wasn't room
for anything but winning. Nothing. Winning was the sole obsession to a fault."

And the fault was defiance of NCAA rules that was "belligerent,
flagrant, and deliberate." The result was two years of probation
for what were called "among the most serious infractions cases
ever processed by the NCAA."

But Pell's legacy is not as simple as probation and disgrace. Bill
Carr, who lost his job as UF athletic director from the Pell fallout,
said, "Charley Pell had the most profound effect of anybody in
UF history next to Steve Spurrier."

When he arrived in Gainesville, Pell found "a fractured fan

base, an athletic department in serious debt, and facilities that were nowhere near what a major college program needed." Florida Field's south end zone was rickety grandstand seating. The weight room and other facilities were "woefully – and even embarrassingly – substandard."

Pell changed all that, championing the construction of a world-class training facility, the expansion of the stadium in the south end zone, and the addition of luxury skyboxes.

While renovations have rendered Florida Field awesome, it will always be subject to further improvements. Our lives, too, can always stand some improvement. We know that; we sometimes try by joining a gym or making New Year's resolutions.

More importantly, though, we must constantly improve ourselves spiritually by becoming more mature in our faith. We can always know more about God's word, discover more ways to serve God, deepen our prayer life and our trust in God, and do a better job of being Jesus to other people through simple acts of kindness and caring.

We are always "under construction" as far as God is concerned because we can always improve our faith life. That is, we can always become more like Jesus. One day we will all stand before God as finished products. We certainly want to present him a mature dwelling, a spiritual mansion, not a hovel.

The principle is competing against yourself. It's about self-improvement, about being better than you were the day before.
-- Former NFL quarterback Steve Young

**Spiritual improvement means a constant effort
to become more like Jesus in our day-to-day lives.**

DAY 54

MIRACLE PLAY

Read Matthew 12:38-42.

"He answered, 'A wicked and adulterous generation asks for a miraculous sign!'" (v. 39)

The 1993 Gators won their second SEC championship, but it took one of the most miraculous plays in history for them even to win their first SEC game.

Florida was heavily favored against Kentucky in Lexington in the Gators' SEC opener, but apparently nobody bothered to tell the Wildcats. With less than a minute to play, Kentucky took a 20-17 lead with what seemed to be a game-winning field goal.

But Harrison Houston gave the Gators hope by returning the kickoff to the Gator 42. Danny Wuerffel then hit wide receiver Jack Jackson and running back Errict Rhett with a couple of quick passes, and suddenly the Gators were sitting on the Kentucky 28 with time running out.

After an incomplete pass, Florida was left with only eight seconds to avoid what Wuerffel said would have been "the biggest upset of the Coach Spurrier era."

The Gators disdained the long field goal and went for the win. Prior to the game Spurrier had extended a scholarship to a walk-on receiver named Chris Doering. Doering rewarded his coach's trust with one of the biggest plays in Gator history.

Spurrier sent four receivers wide, Jackson and Doering to the right, and Aubrey Hill and Houston to the left. Jackson was the intended receiver. He was covered, though, so Wuerffel faked and looked off. He found Doering wide open down the middle and hit him right in the numbers for the miraculous touchdown and a 24-20 win.

"I can't believe it. I really can't," Wuerffel told reporters after the game.

Miracles defy rational explanation. Like scoring a game-winning touchdown on the last play. Or escaping with minor abrasions from an accident that totals your car. Or recovering from an illness that seemed terminal. Underlying the notion of miracles is that they are rare instances of direct divine intervention that reveal God.

But life shows us quite the contrary, that miracles are anything but rare. Since God made the world and everything in it, everything around you is miraculous. Even you are a miracle. Your life can be mundane, dull, and ordinary, or it can be spent in a glorious attitude of childlike wonder and awe. It depends on whether or not you see the world through the eyes of faith; only through faith can you discern the hand of God in any event. Only through faith can you see the miraculous and thus see God.

Jesus knew that miracles don't produce faith, but rather faith produces miracles.

Do you believe in miracles? Yes!
– Broadcaster Al Michaels when U.S. defeated USSR in hockey in
1980 Winter Games

Miracles are all around us, but it takes
the eyes of faith to see them.

DAY 55

NOT WHAT THEY SEEM

Read Habakkuk 1:2-11.

"Why do you make me look at injustice? Why do you tolerate wrong? Destruction and violence are before me; there is strife, and conflict abounds" (v. 3).

The Gators seemed to have lost a baseball game to South Carolina; instead, they had one of their most exciting wins in history.

On April 7, 2007, Florida hosted the Gamecocks in a battle for first place in the SEC East. The Gators sat on top but were only 19-14 for the season while South Carolina was 25-6 and ranked No. 5 in the nation. Carolina led 8-2 in the bottom of the eighth before Brian Leclerc's grand slam – his first home run of the season -- made it 8-6.

The first two Florida batters in the ninth were retired, but Matt LaPorta walked and Bryson Barber was hit by a pitch. That brought sophomore catcher Cody Neer to the plate. Neer's goal was simple: "I was trying to get a base hit." But he fell behind in the count at 1-2; the Gators were down to their last strike.

Neer then blasted a fast ball into deep left-center. The Gamecock centerfielder raced to the wall, jumped, and apparently made a game-winning catch as he slammed into the fence. "I thought he caught it," Neer said. And he did – until he hit the fence. The impact jarred the ball loose. After hesitating, the third-base umpire signaled home run. Florida's dugout emptied and swarmed Neer at home plate.

GATORS

"To our guys credit we kept pushing," said Gators coach Pat McMahon. "This is a heck of a comeback win for our ball club."

Especially after what for a moment seemed to be a Gator loss instead of the 9-8 win.

Sometimes in sports things just aren't what they seem. The same holds true for life also.

In our violent and convulsive times, we must confront the possibility of a new reality: that we are helpless in the face of anarchy; that injustice, destruction, and violence are pandemic in and symptomatic of our modern age. It seems that anarchy is winning, that the system of standards, values, and institutions we have cherished is crumbling while we watch.

But we should not be deceived or disheartened. God is in fact the arch-enemy of chaos, the creator of order and goodness and the architect of all of history. God is in control.

We often misinterpret history as the record of mankind's accomplishments -- which it isn't -- rather than the unfolding of God's plan -- which it is. That plan has a clearly defined end: God will make everything right. In that day things will be what they seem.

Unlike any other business in the United States, sports must preserve an illusion of perfect innocence.

– Author Lewis H. Lapham

**The forces of good and decency often seem
helpless before evil's power, but don't be fooled:
God is in control and will set things right.**

DAY 56

ANSWERING THE CALL

Read 1 Samuel 3:1-18.

"The Lord came and stood there, calling as at the other times, 'Samuel! Samuel!' Then Samuel said, 'Speak, for your servant is listening'" (v. 10).

Wilber Marshall answered the call -- even when he didn't want to.

Marshall was a *Parade* magazine All-American tight end out of high school, and he never wanted to play any other position in college. "Tight end was the world to me," he said. "It was my first dream." Coach Charley Pell told Marshall he could play tight end at Florida, and so he became a Gator. And he did play tight end for one season.

Then in the spring of 1981 Pell asked Marshall to play defense. "We need you on defense. We need help," Pell begged. "We don't have anybody who can play at outside linebacker."

To say the least, Marshall was not particularly delighted with the request: "I was like, 'Hey, wait a minute. I came here to play tight end. This is crazy.'" Marshall spent time by himself to sort everything out; unable to get much sleep or study for his classes, he even considered quitting. "I kept thinking about how I didn't even want to do this anymore," he said.

But then he looked around and saw other guys making changes for the good of the team. "A lot of people were sacrificing," he said, "and I could see it would be best for the team. So I made the switch."

The rest is Gator lore and football history. At outside linebacker, Marshall was a two-time All-America, a three-time All-SEC player, and a first-round NFL draft pick. In 1999, he was named Florida's Defensive Player of the Century.

Wilber Marshall answered the call.

A team player is someone who does whatever the coach calls upon him to do for the good of the team. Something quite similar occurs when God places a specific call upon a Christian's life.

This is much scarier, though, than shifting positions on a football team as Wilber Marshall did. The way many folks understand it is that answering God's call means going into the ministry, packing the family up, and moving halfway around the world to some place where folks have never heard of air conditioning, fried chicken, paved roads, or the Florida Gators. Zambia. The Philippines. Cleveland even.

Not for you, no thank you. And who can blame you?

But God usually calls folks to serve him where they are even when they think living in a particular place was their idea. In fact, God put you where you are right now, and he has a purpose in placing you there.

Wherever you are, God calls you to serve him.

It was like being in a foreign country.
-- Welsh soccer player Ian Rush on playing in Italy

Serving God doesn't necessarily mean entering full-time ministry and going to a foreign land; God calls you to serve him right where you are.

DAY 57

CHEERS

Read Matthew 21:1-11.

"The crowds that went ahead of him and those that followed shouted" (v. 9).

Danny Wuerffel once said that before a Florida game, "you can feel the force of the deafening crowd." It must not have always been like that, though.

Apparently many of the Gator football fans of years ago -- including the students -- sat on their hands a lot during a game if they had a seat at all. The situation got so desperate that before the Stetson game on Friday, Nov. 15, 1912, the student newspaper, the *Florida Alligator*, which was published every Tuesday, urged the students to "yell yourself dumb."

University professors almost certainly sniffed in disapproval, but the editor implored the students to "talk, think, and dream football. If it comes to (cutting) classes or permitting our football spirit to weaken, let the classes slide and make them up after [the game]."

The *Alligator* urged the students to cheer always and never stop no matter what happened. "Let us practice our cheering at every available opportunity and when we get on that field Friday, stick together and yell our lungs out. That's our duty to our college and the way to win games. Furthermore, if the tide of battle seems to be going against us, don't let up on the cheering."

The editor believed student support would be the difference

between winning and losing. "If we do not develop some football and college spirit around this campus, the real stuff, not the poor imitation that we have been putting up, our team, which means our University, is more than likely to go down to defeat."

The earnest exhortations may not have helped, but they certainly didn't hurt. Florida beat Stetson 23-7.

Chances are you go to work every day, do your job well, and then go home to your family. This country couldn't run without you; you're indispensable to the nation's efficiency.

Even so, nobody cheers for you or waves pompoms in your face. Your name probably will never elicit a standing ovation when a PA announcer calls it.

It's just as well, since public opinion is notoriously fickle. Consider what happened to Jesus. When he entered Jerusalem, he was the object of raucous cheering and an impromptu parade. The crowd's adulation reached such a frenzy they tore branches off trees and threw their clothes on the ground.

Five days later the crowd shouted again, only this time they screamed for Jesus' execution.

So don't worry too much about not having your personal set of cheering fans. Remember that you do have one personal cheerleader who will never stop pulling for you: God.

A cheerleader is a dreamer that never gives up.

– Source unknown

Just like the sports stars, you have a personal cheerleader: God.

DAY 58

NO RESPECT

Read Mark 8:31-38.

*"He then began to teach them that the Son of Man must
suffer many things and be rejected by the elders, chief
priests and teachers of the law, and that he must be killed"
(v. 31).*

The Gators showed 'em all right.

The national media said they didn't belong in the 2007 BCS
championship game. Even Las Vegas agreed, installing Florida
as a seven-point underdog to Ohio State. Everybody talked about
how good the Buckeyes were and how they would manhandle
that SEC team that should have playing someplace other than the
Fiesta Bowl. More than a few writers gushed that Ohio State was
one of the best teams in college football history. "Nobody gave us
a chance," wide receiver Dallas Baker said. What nobody gave the
Gators was respect. One newspaper predicted 42-14 Ohio State.

Well, they almost got the score right -- just the wrong team, and
when Florida had finished humiliating Ohio State 41-14, the only
question about the match-up was why anyone had ever thought
the Buckeyes deserved to be in the game. "There's a team that
[didn't] belong in this game" running back Deshawn Wynn said.
"And it's not the Gators." "It ain't disrespect (for Ohio State), it's
the truth," said wide receiver Andre Caldwell.

The way the sports world scoffed at them only made the
players more determined. "Motivation was easy for the last 30

days," Coach Urban Meyer said after the national-championship trophy was headed to Gainesville. "I don't want to say there was a lack of respect, but that's exactly what it was."

The destruction of the highly respected Buckeyes by the disrespected Gators completed a dream season as Florida became the first school in history to be national champions in both football and basketball the same calendar year.

Rodney Dangerfield made a good living as a comedian with a repertoire that was really only countless variations on one punch line: "I don't get no respect." Dangerfield was successful because he struck a chord with his audience. No one wants to be perceived by others as being unworthy of a particular bowl game or a job to which you've been promoted. You want the respect, the honor, the esteem, and the regard that you feel you've earned.

But more often than not, you don't get it. Still, you shouldn't feel too badly; you're in good company. In the ultimate example of disrespect, Jesus – the very Son of God -- was arrested, bound, scorned, ridiculed, spit upon, tortured, condemned, and executed.

As incredible as it sounds, God allowed his son to undergo such treatment because of his high regard and his love for you. You are respected by almighty God! Could anyone else's respect really matter?

Play for your own self-respect and the respect of your teammates.
-- Legendary Vanderbilt coach Dan McGugin

**You may not get the respect you deserve,
but at least nobody's driving nails into you
as they did to Jesus.**

FLORIDA

 DAY 59

A CHANGE OF PLANS

Read Genesis 18:20-33.

"The Lord said, 'If I find fifty righteous people in the city of Sodom, I will spare the whole place for their sake'" (v. 26).

The Gators pulled out the 2006 SEC tournament with a last-second basket because they had a plan -- and didn't execute it.

Florida was not the favorite to win the tournament. In fact, few preseason pundits picked the Gators to do much of anything that season other than be pretty good. With three starters gone and freshman being heavily counted on, 2005-06 was seen as a rebuilding year. Some "experts" picked the Gators to finish as low as fifth in the SEC East.

But there they were on March 12 at the Gaylord Entertainment Center in Nashville playing South Carolina for their second straight tournament title. And there they were tied at 47 with 21 seconds left. The late run, though, had belonged to South Carolina. Florida had led 47-39 with only 4:42 to play, but the Gamecocks proceeded to rip off eight straight points to knot it with only 43 seconds left.

But the Gators had a plan.

Coach Billy Donovan called a time out and instructed his troops on exactly what they were to do. Corey Brewer was to drive to the basket and draw Joakim Noah's defender to him. This would give them two chances: Either Brewer would make the shot or Noah would be in position to grab the rebound and put it back up.

As it turned out, they did neither. Brewer drove, Noah's man moved, and Brewer floated the ball to Noah who banked it in with 11.6 seconds left for the win. The Gators won the championship because they changed their plans.

To be unable to adapt to changing circumstances to is stultify and die. It's true of animal life, of business and industry, of the military, of sports teams, of you and your relationships, your job, and your finances.

Changing your plans regularly therefore is rather routine for you. But consider how remarkable it is that the God of the universe may change his mind about something. What could bring that about?

Prayer. Someone -- an old nomad named Abraham or a 21st-century Florida Gator fan like you -- talks to God, who listens and considers what is asked of him.

You may feel uncomfortable praying. Maybe you're reluctant and embarrassed; perhaps you feel you're not very good at it. But nobody majors in prayer at school, and as for being reluctant, what have you got to lose? Your answer may even be a change of plans on God's part. Such is the power of prayer.

There are two things you can do with your head down: play golf and pray.

-- Lee Trevino

**Prayer is powerful;
it may even change God's mind.**

HEAVEN-BOUND

Read Hebrews 11:13-16.

"They were longing for a better country — a heavenly one" (v. 16a).

Many of us are like Gator offensive tackle Jason Odom: We may be ready to go to Heaven, but we'd just as soon not go right now.

Twice All-SEC and a first-team All America in 1995, Odom was Danny Wuerffel's roommate at Yon Hall; the two became lifelong friends. On the flight home after the 1992 Tennessee game, they feared that their friendship -- and their lives -- might come to a sudden and premature end.

As their plane coasted along at 30,000 feet, the air pressure suddenly dropped. The oxygen masks popped down, and the pilot did what pilots usually do when the oxygen level drops: He went into an emergency descent to 10,000 feet so everyone could resume breathing normally again.

Only, the Gators didn't know this was standard procedure. As Wuerffel put it, "For all we knew, this was a death dive. And no one said anything. Even the flight attendants were scared and nervous. It's not a good thing when the people you're supposed to trust look worried."

Buoyed by his strong faith, Wuerffel remained calm. Just before the dive, the attendants had served everyone food; since he was hungry, Wuerffel decided to eat during the descent by lifting his oxygen mask to take bites of food.

He also put a hand on Odom's shoulder to reassure him and let him know everything would be all right. The move had exactly the opposite effect, however. After the team landed safely, Odom told Wuerffel he was doing just fine until his friend put a hand on his shoulder. I thought you were saying "I love you and I'll see you in Heaven," Odom told him.

Like the Gators flying to games, America is a nation of nomads, packing up the U-Haul and the car and moving on the average about once every five years. We move because we're always seeking something better. Better schools for the kids. A better job. Better weather. Better opportunities.

We're seeking that better place that will make our lives better. Quite often, though, we wind up in a place or in circumstances that are just different, not better. So we try again.

God is very aware of this deep longing in our hearts for something better than what we have now. As only he can, he has made provision for it. What God has prepared for us, however, isn't a place that's just better, but rather a place that is perfect. He has also thoughtfully provided clear directions about how to get there, though we won't get any help from our GPS.

Jesus is the way to that place, that perfect place called Heaven.

When you play a sport, you have two things in mind. One is to get into the Hall of Fame and the other is to go to heaven when you die.
— Lee Trevino

God knows our deep longing for a better place,
so he has prepared one for us: Heaven.

DAY 61

CHANGELESS

Read Hebrews 13:5-16.

"Jesus Christ is the same yesterday and today and forever" (v. 8).

Things have sure changed.

When a team representing what would be the University of Florida played its first game, the school didn't have much money for football. The players, therefore, had to buy their own uniforms, "which consisted of a pair of quilted pants and a light unpadded jersey." Regulation shoes were too expensive for the boys to afford, so most of them "nailed leather cleats to their walking shoes." They didn't wear helmets. Instead, they protected themselves -- somewhat -- "by wearing padded cross straps, which often included nose guards and shin guards." The ball they used was the shape of a watermelon, too big to hold in a hand and pass.

Things were quite different on the field too. A player might hide the ball under his jersey. Spectators often got in the players' way or threw sticks and rocks at the opposing team. Players dragged tackled ball carriers forward. Teams decided upon the length of games once they showed up to play. When dusk threatened, spectators' automobiles were used to light up the field.

This was the wild and wooly game of college football in its early days, the 1890s and the turn of the century. Largely unregulated and unsophisticated, it was a game we would barely recognize today.

Thank goodness, we might well say. Given the symmetry, the excitement, the passion, and the sheer spectacle that surround today's college game, few, if any, Florida fans would long for the days when handles were sewn into uniforms to make ball carriers easier to toss.

Like everything else, football has changed. Computers and CDs, cell phones and George Foreman grills, iPods and IMAX theaters – they and much that is common in your life now may not have even been around when you were 16. Think about how style, cars, communications, and tax laws constantly change.

Don't be too harsh on the world, though, because you've changed also. You've aged, gained or lost weight, gotten married, changed jobs, or relocated.

Have you ever found yourself bewildered by the rapid pace of change, casting about for something to hold on to that will always be the same, that you can use as an anchor for your life? Is there anything like that?

Sadly, the answer's no. All the things of this world change.

On the other hand, there's Jesus, who is the same today, the same forever, always dependable, always loving you. You can grab hold of Jesus and never let go.

I'm not too proud to change. I like to win too much.
-- Bobby Bowden

In our ever-changing and bewildering world,
Jesus is the same forever;
his love for you will never change.

DAY 62

I CAN'T STAND IT!

Read Exodus 32:1-20.

"[Moses'] anger burned and he threw the tablets out of his hands, breaking them to pieces at the foot of the mountain" (v. 19).

So many frustrating Florida football seasons were summed up with one solemn declaration: The Gators couldn't win the big one. Then came Georgia Tech in 1960.

Tech rumbled into Gainesville ranked No. 10; Florida was 2-0 under new head coach Ray Graves with wins over George Washington and FSU. The Gators trailed only 17-10 in the fourth quarter when they took over on their own 15 with 8 ½ minutes left to play. Gator fans didn't know it, but they were about to witness one of the greatest drives and most dramatic finishes in Florida football history.

The Gators moved methodically down the field behind quarterback Larry Libertore and halfback Lindy Infante. Memories of so many years of frustration rose up when the Gators fumbled on third down and left themselves facing fourth and goal at the Tech 4 with the clock ticking down to under a minute. Libertore ran the option and pitched to Infante, who squeezed into the end zone with 32 seconds left. The berserk crowd chanted, "Go for two!" Graves never hesitated; he raised two fingers.

Again, Libertore rolled right, but this time he pulled up and passed to fullback Jon MacBeth for the two-point conversion and the 18-17 win. Thirty years later Graves admitted this was the "biggest game of my career. There were some big ones after that, but that game set the stage for changing the notion that Florida couldn't win the big one." *The Gainesville Sun* declared the win "went a long way toward wiping out years of myriad football frustrations."

The traffic light catches you when you're running late for work or your doctor's appointment. The bureaucrat gives you red tape instead of assistance. Your daughter refuses to take homework seriously. Makes your blood boil, doesn't it?

Frustration is part of God's testing ground that is life even if much of what frustrates us today results from manmade organizations, bureaucracies, and machines. What's important is not that you encounter frustration — that's a given — but how you handle it. Do you respond with curses, screams, and violence? Or with a deep breath, a silent prayer, and calm persistence and patience?

It may be difficult to imagine Jesus stuck in traffic or waiting for hours in a long line in a government office. It is not difficult, however, to imagine how he would act in such situations, and, thus, to know exactly how you should respond. No matter how frustrated you are.

A life of frustration is inevitable for any coach whose main enjoyment is winning.

-- *NFL Hall of Fame Coach Chuck Noll*

Frustration is a vexing part of life,
but God expects us to handle it gracefully.

DAY 63

JUGGERNAUT

Read Revelation 20.

"Fire came down from heaven and devoured them. And the devil, who deceived them, was thrown into the lake of burning sulfur, where the beast and the false prophet had been thrown" (vv. 9b-10a).

When Ole Miss stopped the Gators on fourth and one at the Rebel 32 to clinch a 31-30 upset, even the most die-hard Florida fan could not have foreseen the juggernaut that would be unleashed upon an unsuspecting college football world in 2008.

The Gators had been impressive in their first three wins, burying Hawaii 56-10, defeating Miami 26-3, and proving once again that Rocky Top will always be second in the SEC with a 30-6 romp past Tennessee. After the loss, though, Florida went from impressive to completely dominant.

Consider these scores: 38-7 (Arkansas), 51-21 (4th-ranked LSU), 63-5 (Kentucky), 49-10 (8th-ranked Georgia), 42-14 (Vanderbilt), 56-6 (24th-ranked South Carolina), 70-19 (The Citadel), and 45-15 (FSU).

After losing to Ole Miss, here's what was unleashed:

Florida beat nine opponents – four of which were ranked – by an average of 39.6 points. They finished third in the nation in scoring (45.2 points per game) with quarterback Tim Tebow finishing fifth in the country in passer rating. The Gators led the SEC in rushing, scoring, and total offense. Five running backs averaged more than 40 yards per game.

Florida was equally dominant on the defensive side. Opponents averaged only 12.8 points per game, fifth best in the nation.

It was a run the likes of which the proud old SEC has never seen as the juggernaut that was the 2008 Florida Gators laid complete waste to the conference on their way to the school's eighth SEC title and its third national championship.

Maybe your experience with a juggernaut involved a game against a team full of major college prospects, a league tennis match against a former college player, or your presentation for the project you knew didn't stand a chance. Whatever it was, you've been slam-dunked before.

Being part of a juggernaut is certainly more fun than being in the way of one. Just ask Florida's opponents in 2008. Or consider the forces of evil aligned against God. At least the teams that took the field against the Gators in 2008 had some hope, however slim, that they might win. No such hope exists for those who oppose God.

That's because their fate is already spelled out in detail. It's in the book; we all know how the story ends. God's enemies may talk big and bluster now, but they will be trounced in the most decisive defeat of all time.

You sure want to be on the winning side in that one.

I'd never been to a mercy killing before.
-- New Orleans basketball coach Benny Dees after a 101-76 loss

The most lopsided victory in all of history
is a sure thing: God's ultimate triumph over evil.

DAY 64

CELEBRATION TIME

Read Exodus 14:26-31; 15:19-21.

"Miriam the prophetess, Aaron's sister, took a tambourine in her hand, and all the women followed her, with tambourines and dancing" (v. 15:20).

Though it certainly is not the case now, a football victory over Vanderbilt was once the cause of a massive and joyous celebration by the Gator faithful.

The Gators signaled their commitment to moving into the upper echelons of the SEC by hiring Bob Woodruff as head coach in January 1950. His $17,000 salary was more then either the university's president or Florida's governor made.

The *Florida Alligator* rather poetically stated why such a big-name coach was hired: "It is [Woodruff's] exacting duty to lift (the) University of Florida from the Slough of Despondency and sooner or later, put the so-called Gators into some of the Bowls which yield wide publicity and lavish lucre. Sooner will be better than later." In other words, Woodruff's mission was to win.

The fans' enthusiasm for the new era showed when the Gators upset previously unbeaten Vanderbilt 31-27 in Nashville, which ran Florida's record to 4-1. The *Alligator* reported that when the game ended Gainesville "exploded in an uproar 'unseen here since V-J Day.'" Students took to the streets, car horns blew all night, and a huge victory bonfire at University Avenue and 13th blocked traffic for hours.

GATORS

The celebration continued into the next day when about 15,000 cheering students and fans met the team at the airport to welcome them home. Thousands of cars were stuck on the highway, causing another massive traffic jam.

As the *Alligator* put it, the "wild celebration captured the 'rising pulse of a town caught up in a rare epidemic – football fever.'" Gainesville indeed had football fever -- and celebrated it.

You know what it takes to throw a good party. You start with your closest friends, add some salsa and chips, fire up the grill and throw on some burgers and dogs, and then top it all off with the Florida game on TV.

You probably also know that any old excuse will do to get people together for a celebration. All you really need is a sense that life is pretty good right now.

That's the thing about having Jesus as part of your life: He turns every day into a celebration of the good life. No matter what tragedies or setbacks life may have in store, the heart given to Jesus will find the joy in living. That's because such a life is spent with quiet confidence in God's promise of salvation through Jesus, a confidence that inevitably bubbles up into a joy the troubles of the world cannot touch. When a life is celebrated with Jesus, the party never stops.

Aim high and celebrate that.
> *– Marathon runner Bill Rodgers*

**With Jesus, life is one big party,
a celebration of victory and joy.**

DAY 65

BLIND JUSTICE

Read Micah 6:6-8.

"He has showed you, O man, what is good. And what does the Lord require of you? To act justly and to love mercy and to walk humbly with your God" (v. 8).

What the NCAA did to Florida football in 1990 just wasn't right.

On Sept. 20, during Steve Spurrier's first year as head coach, the NCAA hit the Gators with a two-year probation and a bowl ban for 1990. The penalties were for transgressions that had occurred under Galen Hall. He admitted giving unauthorized payments to two assistant coaches and giving money to a former player for a child support payment. "Human kindness just got kicked in the tail," said defensive coordinator Gary Darnell, who served as interim coach after Hall was fired. "But in our profession, that's sometimes the case because of the rules."

For *that* the Gators were blasted by the NCAA? Not really. Spurrier believed Florida was being penalized again for what had been termed the "belligerent, flagrant, and deliberate" defiance of NCAA rules under Charley Pell for which Florida had already served its sentence. "I'm having a very difficult time accepting this penalty," Spurrier fumed. "The NCAA said it felt it had to do something because of the cheating in '83 and '84. But in America you pay your sentence for one crime and I don't believe you're supposed to pay again six years later."

GATORS

Florida appealed the penalties and offered to cut scholarships in the future in return for the removal of the bowl ban, but to no avail; the injustice stood. The NCAA's heavy-handedness became even more galling when the 1990 team went 9-2 with the best record in the SEC. Because of the penalties, the Gators weren't SEC champions and weren't in the Sugar Bowl.

Where's the justice when cars fly past you just as a state trooper pulls you over? When a con man swindles an elderly neighbor? When crooked politicians treat your tax dollars as their personal slush fund? When children starve?

Injustice enrages us, but anger is not enough. The establishment of justice in this world has to start with each one of us. The Lord requires it of us. For most of us, a just world is one in which everybody gets what he or she deserves.

But that is not God's way. God expects us to be just and merciful in all our dealings without consideration as to whether the other person "deserves" it. The justice we dispense should truly be blind.

If that doesn't sound "fair," then pause and consider that when we stand before God, the last thing we want is what we deserve. We want mercy, not justice.

None of us wants justice from God. What we want is mercy because if we got justice, we'd all go to hell.
-- Bobby Bowden

**God requires that we dispense justice and mercy
without regards to deserts, exactly what we pray
we will in turn receive from God.**

DAY 66

CLOTHES HORSE

Read Genesis 37:1-11.

"Israel loved Joseph more than all his children, because he was the son of his old age: and he made him a coat of many colours" (v. 3 KJV).

Gator legend has it that Larry Smith once scored a touchdown while he was running out of his pants.

From 1966-68, Larry Smith terrorized SEC defenses as a tailback, scoring 24 touchdowns and being named All-SEC first team three times. He led the conference in rushing in 1966 as a sophomore, playing in the backfield with senior quarterback Steve Spurrier. "It was a good year, a fun year," Smith recalled. "It was a pretty good year for the University of Florida."

The Gators went 8-2 that season but were underdogs against eighth-ranked Georgia Tech in the Orange Bowl. They whipped the Jackets solidly, though, 27-12, thanks in large part to one of the greatest and most famous runs in Florida history. The Gators trailed 6-0 and were backed up against their own goal line when Smith took the handoff from Spurrier, hit a hole, cut to his right, and sprinted 94 yards for a game-changing touchdown.

"That play was a bit of a fluke," Smith said. "They were in a goal-line defense and I popped through and there was nobody there. It was a thrill, though."

As Pat Dooley put it in *Game of My Life*, "On television, it appeared that Smith's pants were sliding down as he ran down the sideline for the score. Smith responded it was just "urban legend." "I had these plastic hip pads that were riding up on me," he explained. "Everybody thought my pants were falling down. You can't run with your pants down."

True – but that fact hasn't kept what is perceived as Smith's pants problem from becoming part of Florida football lore.

Contemporary society proclaims that it's all about the clothes. Buy that new suit or dress, those new shoes, and all the sparkling accessories, and you'll be a new person. The changes are only cosmetic, though; under those clothes, you're the same person. Consider Joseph, for instance, prancing about in his pretty new clothes; he was still a spoiled tattletale whose brothers despised him.

Jesus never taught that we should run around half-naked or wear only second-hand clothes from the local mission. He did warn us, though, against making consumer items such as clothes a priority in our lives.

A follower of Christ seeks to emulate Jesus not through material, superficial means such as wearing special clothing like a robe and sandals. Rather, the disciple desires to match Jesus' inner beauty and serenity -- whether the clothes the Christian wears are the sables of a king or the rags of a pauper.

Acquisition of uniforms was up to the team. Each player scrounged for his own quilted pants, jersey, and football shoes.
  – Writer Tom McEwen on the beginning of football at Florida

**Where Jesus is concerned, clothes don't
make the person; faith does.**

DAY 67

AT A LOSS

Read Philippians 3:1-9.

"I consider everything a loss compared to the surpassing greatness of knowing Christ Jesus my Lord, for whose sake I have lost all things" (v. 8).

As long as you are at peace, you don't have to wait for me to come home." With those words, Kim Waleszonia gave her father permission to leave his pain behind.

The 2008 Gator softball team set an NCAA record with 70 wins, won the SEC, and made the program's first-ever trip to the College World Series, advancing to the semifinals.

Waleszonia was a key part of that success. The junior center-fielder was named All-America after a season that featured a .349 batting average and a school record for runs scored. After her junior season, she was Florida's career record holder for batting average, runs, triples, and stolen bases.

But she played all season with a heavy heart. Waleszonia made the decision in August 2007 to give up softball after the family learned her dad was dying of pancreatic cancer. She wanted to help care for her best friend. "He was my life coach," she said. "Softball will be there forever. I told my dad I'd rather spend what I have with you." So she left Florida for California, not knowing whether she would return. "We were prepared not to get her back," said Gator softball coach Tim Walton.

As her father worsened, they talked, and he told his daughter to follow her heart. On Sunday, Jan. 6, 2008, she came back to Florida. He died on Tuesday, at 5:05; he was 49. "My number is five," Waleszonia said. "I feel like that was his sign for me."

As for the season in the wake of the loss, "I look at my numbers and wonder how it's possible," she said. "That's how much I feel like I've struggled."

Maybe, as it was with Kim Waleszonia, it was when a family member died. Perhaps it wasn't so staggeringly tragic: your puppy died, your best friend moved away, or an older sibling left home. Sometime in your youth or early adult life, though, you learned that loss is a part of life.

Loss inevitably diminishes your life, but loss and the grief that accompanies it are part of the price of loving. When you first encountered loss, you learned that you were virtually helpless to prevent it or escape it.

There is life after loss, though, because you have one sure place to turn. Jesus can share your pain and ease your suffering, but he doesn't stop there. Through the loss of his own life, he has transformed death -- the ultimate loss -- into the ultimate gain of eternal life. In Jesus lies the promise that one day loss itself will die.

To win, you have to risk loss.

-- *Olympic champion skier Jean-Claude Killy*

Jesus not only eases the pain of our losses
but transforms the loss caused by death
into the gain of eternal life.

DAY 68

GOOD AS ONE'S WORD

Read Matthew 12:33-37.

*"For out of the overflow of the heart the mouth speaks.
The good man brings good things out of the good stored
up in him, and the evil man brings evil things out of the
evil stored up in him" (vv. 34b-35).*

For four decades, Gator fans seeking to hear the word on the Gators turned to one man: Otis Boggs.

Boggs was the "Voice of the Gators" in an age before omnipresent television when radio was the only medium for sports broadcasting. Generations of Gator fans counted on Boggs to watch the game for them and connect them to the action with his "gentle, melodious voice."

Boggs knew early on that he wanted to get into radio, coming to Gainesville in part because the university had a radio station. He began his Gator broadcasting career in 1939 as a student, often using what was called a re-creation broadcast because the station couldn't afford to send anyone to the road games. "We would get the Western Union to supply the very bare information about who carried the ball, where he was tackled, and you had to ad lib and make up a picture. Sound effects were put in," Boggs recalled.

Through 42 years of Florida games – through good times and bad times – his approach was always the same: He was a professional. "I never did any of that 'our, mine, we' stuff," he once said. "But I think that most anyone who listened to Otis Boggs

GATORS

broadcasting a football game certainly would tell you he was pro-Florida. . . . . But I never believed in saying 'my Gators' or 'our Gators.' I also never believed in putting down the other team."

Boggs' "syrupy Southern style" left the booth when he retired after the 1981 season. With him went an era in Florida football when the words painted the picture.

These days, everybody's got something to say and likely as not a place to say it. Talk radio, 24-hour sports and news TV channels, *Oprah*, *The View*. Talk has really become cheap.

But words still have power, and that includes not just those of the talking heads, hucksters, and pundits on television, but ours also. Our words are perhaps the most powerful force we possess for good or for bad. The words we speak today can belittle, wound, humiliate, and destroy. They can also inspire, heal, protect, and create. Our words both shape and define us. They also reveal to the world the depth of our faith.

We should never make the mistake of underestimating the power of the spoken word. After all, speaking the Word was the only means Jesus had to get his message across – and look what he managed to do.

We must always watch what we say, because others sure will.

My daddy always taught me these words: care and share.
– Tiger Woods

Choose your words carefully; they are the most powerful force you have for good or for bad.

A MOTHER'S LOVE

Read John 19:25-30.

"Near the cross of Jesus stood his mother" (v. 25).

Pam Tebow was willing to die for her son. Literally.

She and her husband Bob already had four children when they prayed for a fifth while they served as missionaries in the Philippines, sharing their faith with the natives and building a ministry.

Their prayers were answered, but just before her pregnancy, Pam fell into a coma from bacteria in some contaminated drinking water. The medical treatment included a series of strong medications. She recovered completely and stopped her medical regimen when she discovered she was pregnant, but the doctors told her the damage had been done. The fetus would be stillborn, they said, and the pregnancy would also endanger her life. The doctors urged her to abort.

"They thought I should have an abortion to save my life from the beginning all the way through the seventh month," she recalled. But for Pam the decision to carry on with the pregnancy was a simple one because of her faith. "We were grieved," she said, but Bob and she "just prayed that if the Lord would give us a son, that he would let us raise him."

In the seventh month, she went to Manila for round-the-clock care. For two months, she remained on bed rest and steadfastly prayed for a healthy child. On Aug. 14, 1987, her due date, she gave birth to a "skinny but rather long" boy who was healthy except for some malnourishment, which he definitely made up for.

They named him Timothy. Tim Tebow: the son his mother was willing to die for.

Mamas often do the sorts of thing Pam Tebow did: risk their own health or sacrifice their personal happiness for the sake of their children. No mother in history, though, has faced a challenge to match that of Mary, whom God chose to be the mother of Jesus. Like mamas and their children throughout time, Mary experienced both joy and perplexity in her relationship with her son.

To the end, though, Mary stood by her boy. She followed him all the way to his execution, an act of love and bravery since Jesus was condemned as an enemy of the Roman Empire.

But just as mothers like Mary and Pam Tebow – and perhaps yours -- would apparently do anything for their children, so will God do anything out of love for his children. After all, that was God on the cross at the foot of which Mary stood, and he was dying for you, one of his children.

Everyone should find time to write and to go see their mother. I think that's healthy.

— *Bear Bryant*

**Mamas often sacrifice for their children,
but God, too, will do anything out of love
for his children, including dying on a cross.**

DAY 70

PLAYING BY THE RULES

Read Luke 5:27-32.

"Why do you eat and drink with tax collectors and 'sinners'?" (v. 30b)

The Gators once played a football game in which *every* touchdown was illegal.

In 1924, Florida went west to Austin to play the University of Texas. The game ended in a 7-7 tie, and according to Gen. James A. Van Fleet, who was the Gator coach, both the scores were achieved by breaking the rules.

The trip to Texas was unpopular because it took the students out of class for most of the week. Football enthusiast Judge Robert Cockrel traveled with the team ostensibly to hold daily classes. But, as Van Fleet put it, "After the first attempt the judge surrendered."

Texas scored its touchdown after the whistle blew for the end of the first half. According to Van Fleet, "The horn actually blew *before* the ball was placed in play." Florida's score was achieved through a rules violation that was much less blatant, but the touchdown was illegal nevertheless.

Van Fleet recalled that the Gator right end, Joe Merrin, lined up to the left of the regular left end, Pete Leitsey. Quarterback Edgar Jones then passed to Leitsey for a touchdown, but because of where Merrin had lined up, Leitsey was in effect the left tackle and was therefore an ineligible receiver. The referees didn't catch it, and when Leitsey lined up in his regular position for the extra point, everything looked just fine to the officials.

Van Fleet confessed he never really felt bad about what he called "that cheat," but "I really believe Preacher Ullysses Gordon will ask forgiveness of the good Lord."

You live by rules others set up. Some lender determined the interest rate on your mortgage and your car loan. You work hours and shifts somebody else established. Someone else decided what day your garbage gets picked up and what school district your house is in.

Jesus encountered societal rules also, including a strict set that dictated what company he should keep, what people in other words, were fit for him to socialize with, talk to, or share a meal with. Jesus ignored the rules, choosing love instead and demonstrating both his love and his disdain for society's rules by mingling with the outcasts, the lowlifes, the poor, and the misfits.

You, too, have to choose when you find yourself in the presence of someone whom society deems undesirable. Will you choose the rules or love? Are you willing to be a rebel for love — as Jesus was?

The rules were a bit sketchy. Against Alabama, we grabbed each other by the belt to prevent the runner from coming between us.
— FAC lineman William Morrow Rowlett Jr. (1903)

Society's rules dictate who is acceptable
and who is not, but love in the name of Jesus
knows no such distinctions.

THE LEADER

Read Matthew 16:13-19.

"You are Peter, and on this rock I will build my church, and the gates of Hades will not overcome it" (v. 18).

In Florida's march to the BCS national championship in 2006, the 42-0 romp over Central Florida in the second game of the season may seem like an insignificant blip on the season's radar screen. But that game may well have been the one that defined -- and made possible -- the incredible season.

The story of the game was quarterback Chris Leak, whose play was described as "near-flawless." He threw for 352 yards and four touchdowns, but the stats don't really tell the story of what happened that day.

What Coach Urban Meyer saw was the verification of what he had been saying all summer: Chris Leak was a better quarterback -- and most importantly, a better leader -- than he had been the season before.

Leak had shown himself to be such a capable leader that Meyer turned part of the offense over to him. "Chris comes in on Sunday and Thursday and he actually scripts the offense for us for the first 12 plays of the game," Meyer said. "That's Chris Leak's offense now."

"I'm real comfortable in the offense," Leak said. "Coach Meyer gave me the keys to the offense. It's given me confidence. I try to get around to everybody to see what they like and how they feel about certain plays. I go off that and script the plays with the coaches giving me input." In other words, Chris Leak was being the team's leader, getting about the business of leading them all the way to the national championship.

Every aspect of life that involves people – every organization, every group, every project, every team -- must have a leader. If goals are to be reached, somebody must take charge.

Even the early Christian church was no different. Jesus knew this, so he designated the leader in Simon Peter, who was, in fact, quite an unlikely choice to assume such an awesome, world-changing responsibility. In *Twelve Ordinary Men*, John MacArthur described Simon as "ambivalent, vacillating, impulsive, unsub-missive." Hardly a man to inspire confidence in his leadership skills. Yet, Peter became, according to MacArthur, "the greatest preacher among the apostles" and the "dominant figure" in the birth of the church.

The implication for your own life is obvious and unsettling. You may think you lack the attributes necessary to make a good leader for Christ. But consider Simon Peter, an ordinary man who allowed Christ to rule his life and became the foundation upon which the Christian church was built.

All the guys who played with him still root for him. Steve Spurrier was the leader.
— *Florida running back Larry Smith (1966-68)*

God's leaders are men and women
who allow Jesus to lead them.

DAY 72

HEART OF THE MATTER

Read Matthew 6:19-24.

"Store up for yourselves treasures in heaven . . . . For where your treasure is, there your heart will be also" (vv. 20, 21).

Billy Donovan followed his heart -- and it led him back to Gainesville.

In the spring of 2007 after coaching the Gators to two straight national championships, Donovan was offered the job as head coach of the Orlando Magic. The move made perfect sense. The Magic were a playoff team with a franchise player and salary cap money to play with. The money involved was generous: almost $5 million a year for five years. As Donovan put it, "If I wanted to try the NBA, this was the time, and the situation was as good as I was likely to get."

As he always does when he faces a touch decision, Donovan sat down and made a list, and when he finished, the positives of making the move outweighed the negatives. So he took the job and announced his decision at press conferences in Orlando and Gainesville.

But as he drove home, Donovan realized "something inside me didn't feel right." He looked over to his wife, Christine, and said, "I'm not so sure I didn't just make a mistake." The more he thought about not coaching Florida, the more unhappy he became.

What in the world? Didn't all the dictates of logic and reason convince him to make the move? They did, but Donovan knew more was involved than cold facts. "I realized that the one thing you can't put on paper is what you feel in your heart," he said. "My heart was telling me Florida was where I belonged."

He followed his heart, changed his mind, and stayed in Gainesville.

As Billy Donovan did, we often face decisions in life that force us to choose between our heart and our head. Our head says take that job with the promotion and the salary increase; our heart says don't relocate because the kids are doing so well. Our head declares now is not the time to start a relationship; our heart insists that we're in love.

We wrestle with our head and our heart as we determine what matters the most to us. When it comes to the ultimate priority in our lives, though, our head *and* our heart tell us it's Jesus.

What that means for our lives is a resolution of the conflict we face daily: That of choosing between the values of our culture and a life of trust in and obedience to God. The two may occasionally be compatible, but when they're not, our head tells us what Jesus wants us to do; our heart tells us how right it is that we do it.

If it's something that you really want to do in your heart, stick with it and work hard and just keep your faith in Christ.
— All-Pro defensive back Ty Law

**In our struggle with competing value systems,
our head and our heart lead us to follow Jesus.**

PEACEMONGERS

Read Hebrews 12:14-17.

"Make every effort to live in peace with all men and to be holy" (v. 14).

After the first pass Carlos Alvarez caught as a Gator, he started a fight -- in practice.

"All of my Cuban temper came up," Florida's greatest pass receiver ever explained about his pugilistic beginning as a Gator receiver.

Alvarez caught only one pass his senior season at North Miami High where he played running back and safety, the positions for which Florida recruited him. He weighed only 175 pounds when he arrived in Gainesville, and he began to question if running back were the right position for him when he saw 200-pound All-American running back Larry Smith in action. "If that's the style of Florida football," he thought, "I'll be dead by the end of the first year."

So the Gators moved him to wide receiver, and he prepared for the position change with a strenuous off-season workout schedule. One of his first routes at practice was a post pattern. Alvarez caught a perfect spiral from John Reaves and slowed down -- only to have All-American defensive back Steve Tannen level him from behind. "I beat Tannen clean, John threw a perfect pass, but Tannen came behind me when I stopped and just killed me," Alvarez recalled.

He immediately, jumped on Tannen and started a fight. "The coaches were all over me, telling me you're not supposed to do that with the varsity." But Coach Lindy Infante, who had recruited Alvarez, sidled over to him and said, "Don't do that . . . but he deserved it."

One day at practice – and Alvarez knew he was going to be a wide receiver for Florida.

Perhaps you've never been in a brawl or a public brouhaha or even rared back and slugged someone. But maybe you retaliated when you got one elbow too many in a pickup basketball game. Or maybe you and your spouse or your teenager get into it occasionally, shouting and saying cruel things. Or road rage and some unseemly gestures may be a part of your life.

While we certainly do seem to live in a more belligerent, confrontational society than ever before, fighting is still not the solution to a problem. Fighting serves only to escalate the whole confrontation, leaving wounded pride, intransigence, and simmering hatred in its wake. Actively seeking and making peace is the way to a solution that lasts and heals.

Peacemaking is not as easy as fighting, but it is much more courageous and a lot less painful. It is also the Jesus thing to do.

In 1903, when the game began, I suggested to the player opposite me that if he would not slug me, I would not slug him.
– FAC lineman William Morrow Rowlett Jr.

Making peace instead of fighting takes courage and strength, but it's certainly the less painful option.

DAY 74

IMPRESSIONS

Read Mark 6:1-6.

"And [Jesus] was amazed at their lack of faith" (v. 6).

Offensive coordinator Dan Mullen made an indelible impression on his players – and it wasn't for anything he did on the practice field or at the blackboard.

At Florida's team meeting the Friday night before the game against Auburn on Saturday, Sept. 29, 2007, Mullen realized something was wrong. Rather than going away, a pain in his abdomen was worsening. So after dinner and the team's walk-through, Mullen went to Shands Hospital. By 1 a.m. Saturday, he was undergoing an emergency appendectomy.

Incredibly, he not only did not miss the game that day, he was on the job, calling the plays. After being released from the hospital around mid-morning, he rejoined the team and even quit taking his pain medication so he could be clear-headed.

Mullen never even considered missing the game. "I just sucked it up and went," he said after Monday's practice, still walking gingerly. "I was pretty determined to be there." He waved off any assertions about how tough he was. "Once the game starts, you are filled with a lot of adrenaline," Mullen said.

His players weren't buying it; quarterback Tim Tebow, for one, was impressed. "He was a warrior," Tebow said, dumbfounded that Mullen actually apologized to him for messing up his pre-game routine. "He didn't mess anything up. He gave us motivation."

Center Drew Miller was another Gator whom Mullen impressed with his grittiness. "It was scary," Miller said. Coach Mullen is "a competitor and a warrior to get back out there just like a player would. I'm proud to have a coach that does stuff like that."

You bought that canary convertible mainly to impress the girls; a white Accord would transport you more efficiently. You seek out subtle but effective ways to gain the boss' approval. You may be all grown up now, but you still want your parents' favor. You dress professionally but strikingly and take your prospective clients to that overpriced steak house.

In our lives we are constantly seeking to impress someone else so they'll remember us and respond favorably to us. That's exactly the impression we should be making upon Jesus because in God's scheme for salvation, only the good opinion of Jesus Christ matters. On that fateful day when we stand before God, all eternity will rest upon Jesus' remembering and responding favorably to us.

We don't want to be like the folks in Jesus' hometown. Oh, they impressed him all right: with their lack of faith in him. This is not the impression we want to make.

I broke in with four hits and the writers declared they had seen the new Ty Cobb. It took me only a few days to correct that impression.
—Casey Stengel

**Jesus is the only one worth impressing,
and it is the depth of your faith – or the lack of it –
that impresses him.**

DAY 75

THE WINNING FORMULA

Read 1 John 1:5-10.

"If we confess our sins, he is faithful and just and will forgive us our sins and purify us from all unrighteousness" (v. 9).

At Florida, Steve Spurrier brought an unprecedented level of offensive sophistication to the college game that had opposing coaches scrambling to catch up. In stark contrast, his overall coaching philosophy in regards to the game itself and to his players was surprisingly simple.

Spurrier's record as the head Gator speaks for itself. From 1990-2001, Spurrier coached the Gators to football success "few supporters of the program dared to dream about." His teams won six SEC titles and the 1996 national championship. He won 122 games in his twelve years at the helm while losing only 27 times; every one of his teams was ranked in the top 15. He is generally "credited with changing the way the SEC played offense," employing "a pass-oriented offense in contrast to the ball control, rush-oriented offenses that were traditionally found in the SEC." His offensive scheme was frequently described as "innovative," forcing "many in the conference to change their offensive and defensive play calling."

And yet through it all, Spurrier's approach to what it took to win and what he demanded from his players remained remarkably simple. "It is our job as coaches to teach and develop player skills. What we expect from the players is effort and concentration," he once said. "I and my entire staff look for and emphasize the positive. That's our approach to building pride, togetherness, dedication and a family atmosphere."

Teaching, effort, concentration, a positive attitude: That was Steve Spurrier's amazingly simple formula for the astounding success he and his teams enjoyed at Florida.

Perhaps the simple life in America was doomed by the arrival of the programmable VCR. Since then, we seem to have been on an inevitably downward spiral into ever more complicated lives. Even windshield wipers have multiple settings now.

We would do very well, however, to mimic in our own lives Steve Spurrier's very basic approach to football. That is, we should approach our lives with the keen awareness that success requires simplicity, a sticking to the basics: Revere God, love your family, honor your country, do your best.

Theologians may make what God did in Jesus as complicated as quantum mechanics and the infield fly rule, but God kept it simple for us: believe, trust, and obey. Believe in Jesus as the Son of God, trust that through him God makes possible our deliverance from our sins into Heaven, and obey God in the way he wants us to live.

That's the true winning formula.

I think God made it simple. Just accept Him and believe.
-- Bobby Bowden

**Life continues to get ever more complicated,
but God made it simple for us
when he showed up as Jesus.**

DAY 76

TEN TO REMEMBER

Read Exodus 20:1-17.

"God spoke all these words: 'I am the Lord your God . . . .
You shall have no other gods before me'" (vv. 1, 3).

Not surprisingly, the Florida Gators have had quite a few laughers during their long and storied football history.

They will probably never match the whipping they put on Southern College, which later became Florida Southern, in the 1913 season opener. The Gators scored 22 touchdowns in 48 minutes to win 144-0. They set one dubious record that will certainly never be broken when they missed ten extra points. End/quarterback George Moseley scored two touchdowns and "never missed a tackle" on defense.

Florida has put some pretty solid whippings on other teams over the years. In 1912, they buried the College of Charleston 78-0 and were "hard put to keep from skyrocketing the score." In 1924, the Gators rolled past Rollins 77-0.

All the lopsided scores weren't rolled up in the early days, though. In 1997, Florida destroyed Central Michigan 82-6. Mercer was subjected to the Gator chomp in 1928, losing 73-0 to what still ranks among the finest Florida teams ever. The squad came within a one-point loss of a shot at the national championship. The Gators rolled up an incredible 805 yards in the Mercer game with halfback Tommy Owens scoring four touchdowns.

Other games among the ten worst defeats the Gators have

handed out are a 69-0 romp over Montana State in the 1988 season opener, a 73-7 slaughter of the Kentucky Wildcats in 1994, and a trio of 65-0 wins, over Rollins in 1925, Cal State-Fullerton in 1987, and Kentucky in 1996.

For Gator fans, this is indeed a list of ten games to remember for the ages.

You've got your list and you're ready to go: a gallon of paint and a water hose from the hardware store; chips, peanuts, and sodas from the grocery store for tonight's card game with your buddies; the tickets for the band concert. Your list helps you remember.

God made a list once of things he wanted you to remember: the Ten Commandments. Just as your list reminds you to do something, so does God's list remind you of how you are to act in your dealings with other people and with him.

A life dedicated to Jesus is a life devoted to relationships, and God's list emphasizes that the social life and the spiritual life of the faithful cannot be sundered. God's relationship to you is one of unceasing, unqualified love, and you are to mirror that divine love in your relationships with others.

In case you forget, you have a list.

Society today treats the Ten Commandments as if they were the ten suggestions. Never compromise on right or wrong.
-- College baseball coach Gordie Gillespie

God's list is a set of instructions on how you are to conduct yourself with other people and with him.

DAY 77

THE PRIZE

Read Philippians 3:10-16.

"I press on toward the goal to win the prize for which God has called me heavenward in Christ Jesus" (v. 14).

What Steve Spurrier did with his Heisman Trophy changed the way the trophy is presented.

When Spurrier won college football's greatest award back in 1966, times were different. The votes came in on Nov. 23, and so for weeks ahead of the presentation in New York City, Spurrier knew he had won the award. The New York ceremony was thus nothing more than a formality unlike today's procedure when the winner's name is a closely guarded secret until the moment of the announcement. The trophy presentation wasn't the media circus it is today; in fact, TV cameras weren't even present for Spurrier's acceptance.

After officials from the Downtown Athletic Club presented him the prize, Spurrier called University of Florida President J. Wayne Reitz forward and told him, "This trophy doesn't belong to me. This belongs to the University of Florida." He then handed the surprised president "college football's most coveted piece of hardware." "I want to present this trophy to the University of Florida where students and alumni can see it if they so desire," Spurrier said.

The gesture prompted the Gator student body to raise funds and to petition the Downtown Athletic Club to issue a second

Heisman Trophy that they would pay for and present to Spurrier. Moved by Spurrier's magnanimity and the response of the Florida students, the club made another trophy and gave it to Spurrier for his personal trophy case.

Ever since then, the club issues two Heisman trophies annually, one for the school to have and display and one for the winning athlete to keep.

Even the most modest among us can't help but be pleased by prizes and honors. They are tangible and visible symbols of the approval and appreciation of others, whether it's an Employee of the Month trophy, a plaque for sales achievement, or the sign declaring yours as the neighborhood's prettiest yard.

Awards and prizes are nice. The danger they present is the possibility that they will become the goal. It's like a football player padding his own statistics to win postseason awards at the expense of victories for his team.

In our pursuit of personal achievement, accomplishment, and the approbation of a fawning world, we must be careful never to take our eyes off the greatest prize of all. It's one that the world can't offer us. It also won't rust, won't collect dust, and won't leave us wondering why we worked so hard to win it in the first place.

It's eternal life, and it's ours through Jesus Christ.

A gold medal is a wonderful thing, but if you're not enough without it, you'll never be enough with it.

-- *John Candy in* Cool Running

The greatest prize of all doesn't require competition to claim it; God has it ready to hand to you through Jesus Christ.

DAY 78

GOOD SPORTS

Read Titus 2:1-8.

*"Show integrity, seriousness and soundness of speech that
cannot be condemned, so that those who oppose you may
be ashamed because they have nothing bad to say about
us" (vv. 7b, 8).*

The 2007 Florida baseball team had a win in the bag, but they refused to take it because they considered doing so to be poor sportsmanship.

In the April 22, 2007, game against Kentucky, the Gators were three minutes away from a home win. Because of the SEC's travel policy and Kentucky's 5:45 p.m. flight out of Jacksonville, the teams couldn't start an inning after 2:15 p.m. The Gators had to kill only nine minutes when they came to bat in the bottom of the eighth at 2:06 p.m. leading 3-2.

But Florida refused to drag around. Coach Pat McMahon said he doesn't believe it is ethical for a team to purposefully stall to secure a win. "The integrity of the game is very important to me," he said. "I feel very strongly about that. We play the game the way it should be played."

The Gators made two quick outs and then put together three straight singles including an Austin Pride RBI that made the score 4-2. That brought Brian Leclerc to the plate at 2:12 p.m. He flied out, and Kentucky got one more at-bat. "We're not the kind of team that's going to milk the clock," Leclerc said. "We want to win the right way. We don't want to win that way. We're better than that."

The Wildcats promptly rallied and tied the game in the ninth on a two-out hit. Florida's insistence on ethics and sportsmanship paid off, though, when Chris Petrie slapped a bases-loaded single in the bottom of the ninth to score Avery Barnes and secure the 5-4 win.

One of life's paradoxes is that many who would never consider cheating on the tennis court or the racquetball court to gain an advantage think nothing of doing so in other areas of their life. In other words, the good sportsmanship they practice on the golf course or even on the Monopoly board doesn't carry over. They play with the truth, cut corners, abuse others verbally, run rough-shod over the weaker, and generally cheat whenever they can to gain an advantage on the job or in their personal relationships.

But good sportsmanship is a way of living, not just of playing. Shouldn't you accept defeat without complaint (You don't have to like it.); win gracefully without gloating; treat your competition with fairness, courtesy, generosity, and respect? That's the way one team treats another in the name of sportsmanship. That's the way one person treats another in the name of Jesus.

One person practicing sportsmanship is better than a hundred teaching it.

-- Knute Rockne

Sportsmanship -- treating others with courtesy, fairness, and respect -- is a way of living, not just a way of playing.

DAY 79

CLOCKWORK

Read Matthew 25:1-13.

"Keep watch, because you do not know the day or the hour" (v. 13).

Florida once whipped LSU after time had apparently run out.

The Gators were 3-1 with the nation's top-ranked defense when they played LSU in Baton Rouge on Oct. 7, 1989. All the drama wasn't on the field as during the week, Florida officials had met with head coach Galen Hall and told him the LSU game would be his last.

The defenses dominated with Florida eking out a 3-0 lead at halftime. In the last half, LSU broke a swing pass for a score and Emmitt Smith popped a 25-yard run for a TD. The score was tied at 13 with 1:20 left when Florida moved methodically down the field behind pinpoint passing from quarterback Kyle Morris.

Hoping to cross up the LSU defense, Florida ran a draw but Smith didn't get out of bounds. Morris hurried the offense to the line as the clock ticked away the final seconds. He hurriedly threw the ball out of bounds, but the clock showed nothing but zeroes. Brad Culpepper, an All-American defensive tackle in 1991, recalled that LSU's fans "started celebrating like they had won the game when it was really tied. I found that strange."

But Hall cornered the officials and argued that there was a second left on the clock. The officials huddled and agreed. In one of those strange but fortuitous decisions coaches make, Arden

Czyzewski, rather than regular kicker John David Francis, was sent in to attempt a 41-yard field goal. "We were all wondering why John David wasn't out there," Culpepper said.

As the Gator nation held its breath, Cryzewski "made it by the skin of his teeth," and the Gators had a stunning 16-13 win – after time had run out. As LSU had done earlier, Florida now started "celebrating like crazy."

We may pride ourselves on our time management, but the truth is that we don't manage time; it manages us. Hurried and harried, we live by schedules that seem to have too much what and too little when. By setting the bedside alarm at night, we even let the clock determine how much down time we get. A life of leisure actually means one in which time is of no importance.

Every second of our life – all the time we have – is a gift from God, who dreamed up time in the first place. We would do well, therefore, to consider what God considers to be good time management. After all, Jesus himself warned us against mismanaging the time we have.

From God's point of view, using our time wisely means being prepared at every moment for Jesus' return, which will occur -- well, only time will tell when.

We didn't lose the game; we just ran out of time.
                                    – Vince Lombardi

**We mismanage our time when we fail
to prepare for Jesus' return even though
we don't know when that will be.**

DAY 80

THE FUNERAL

Read Romans 6:3-11.

"If we died with Christ, we believe that we will also live with him" (v. 8).

Tearful and joyful was how Tom Jones' funeral was described.

Jones was the head coach of Florida's women's track and field team. He died of cancer at 62 in March 2007, and more than 500 people gathered at his funeral to celebrate the man and his life.

Jones enjoyed a 35-year coaching career, the last 15 heading up the Gator women. His tenure in Gainesville was marked by unqualified success. His teams won six SEC championships and fifteen times finished in the top ten at the NCAA Indoor and Outdoor Championships. He was named the NCAA Women's National Indoor Coach of the Year in 1997 and 2002 and the NCAA Outdoor Coach of the Year in 1997. Those he coached also enjoyed success in the classroom with 224 of his Gator athletes being named to the SEC Academic Honor Roll.

But those who spoke of him at his funeral remembered Jones as much more than a track coach. For instance, Florida athletics director Jeremy Foley said, "Most of all, Tom Jones was a good person. At the University of Florida, you will be missed. We were honored you were our coach."

The day was certainly tearful as family members, friends, coworkers, and athletes remembered a man whom they loved.

But joyful? How could it be a joyful day?

One of Jones' former athletes, Olympic gold medalist Maicel Malone, the head women's track coach at Florida A&M, explained how the day could be joyous: "The angels now rejoice in his arrival. God has now welcomed him home."

Chances are you won't get the kind of send-off Tom Jones had with college coaches, athletic directors, and Olympic gold medalists gathering to sing your praises. Still, you want a good funeral. You want a decent crowd, you want folks to shed some tears, and you want some reasonably distinguished-looking types to stand behind a lectern and say some nice things about you. Especially if they're all true.

But have you ever been to a funeral where the deceased you knew and the deceased folks were talking about were two different people? Where everyone struggled to say something nice about the not-so-dearly departed? Or a funeral that was little more than an empty acknowledgement that death is the end of all hope. Sad, isn't it?

Exactly what does make a good funeral, one where people laugh, love, and remember warmly and sincerely amid their tears? Jesus does. His presence transforms a mourning of death into a celebration of life.

Always go to other people's funerals; otherwise, they won't come to yours.

-- Yogi Berra

**Amid tears there is hope; amid death there is
resurrection – if Jesus is at the funeral.**

DAY 81

WHAT YOU GOTTA DO

Read 2 Samuel 12:1-15a.

"The Lord sent Nathan to David" (v. 1).

Linebacker Scot Brantley was twice All-SEC at Florida and played eight seasons in the NFL with Tampa Bay, so in his life he has known all about doing what you have to do to succeed. But one of the hardest things he ever had to do was to tell someone he was going to play football for the Gators.

Brantley was not one of those players who are unknown in high school, get few scholarship offers, and surprise everyone by making it big-time at a major university. The recruiting letters started coming in 1973 during his sophomore season of high school after he started as a freshman at Ocala Forest High.

From the first, Brantley leaned toward the Gators, but he listened when Bear Bryant and Woody Hayes showed up at his home. "Nobody from my county ever had a chance to play for coaches like that," Brantley said. He visited Georgia and Tennessee, but the choice finally came down to Florida and Alabama. "I remember Bear Bryant calling me every Wednesday night for a year and a half," Brantley said. "You could put your hand on the phone and it would ring at 6 p.m. every Wednesday night." Curley Hallman recruited Brantley for Alabama, and "We really hit it off." Bryant sent him a picture and wrote on it, "We're counting on you at 'Bama."

Still, Florida's lure was too strong. When Brantley told Hallman of his decision, the coach said there was no way he was going to break the news to Bryant. "Curley told me, 'I'm not calling him. You tell him,'" Brantley said.

And so he did what he had to do even though it wasn't easy. "I cried when I talked to him," Brantley said.

You've also had to do some things in your life that you just flat didn't want to do. Maybe when you put your daughter on severe restriction, broke the news of a death in the family, fired a friend, or underwent surgery. You plowed again because you knew it was for the best or you had no choice.

Nathan surely didn't want to confront King David and tell him what a miserable reprobate he'd been, but the prophet had no choice: Obedience to God overrode all other factors.

Of all that God asks of us in the living of a godly life, obedience is perhaps the most difficult. After all, our history of disobedience stretches all the way back to the Garden of Eden. The problem is that God expects obedience not only when his wishes match our own but also when they don't.

Obedience to God is a way of life; it is never just a matter of convenience.

Coaching is making men do what they don't want, so they can become what they want to be.
-- Legendary NFL Coach Tom Landry

You can never foresee what God will demand of you, but obedience requires being ready to do whatever God asks.

DAY 82

TEST CASE

Read 1 Peter 4:12-16.

"Do not be surprised at the painful trial you are suffering, as though something strange were happening to you" (v. 12).

They were tested -- and they were not found wanting.

Doug Dickey's 1971 Gator football team finished only 4-7. "We've been snakebit something awful," was Dickey's lament about that team that could just never get it going. Whatever problems or shortcomings the players may have had, character wasn't among them. For one magnificent afternoon with their season already in shambles, they rose up to show their fans exactly what they were made of.

The team was hit hard by injuries. All-world receiver Carlos Alvarez, for instance, was never healthy. They were also plagued by turnovers, committing twelve in the first two games. As a result, they started the season 0-5. But defensive tackle Robert Harrell spoke for the team when he declared, "We are not going to quit. . . . [Q]uite the contrary. We are going to explode and when we do, watch out."

If ever the Gators had a chance to just mail it in, it was the Florida State game. The Seminoles came in undefeated and ranked No. 19: 5-0 vs. 0-5. But the Gators surprised the Noles with a ground attack as quarterback John Reaves threw only eleven passes. Mike Rich hurdled a pile of players to score the first

Florida rushing touchdown of the season, and the Gators played inspired defense against FSU quarterback Gary Huff. The result was one of the great upsets in Gator history as Florida won 17-15 and Dickey enjoyed a victory ride on his players' shoulders.

The Gators' character and will had been tested, and their response left no doubts as to what kind of men the players and coaches were.

Life often seems to be one battery of tests after another: high-school and college final exams, college entrance exams, the driver's license test, professional certification exams. They all stress us out because they measure our competency, and we fear that we will be found wanting.

But it is the tests in our lives that don't involve paper and pen that often demand the most of us. That is, like the Florida football team of 1971, we regularly run headlong into challenges, obstacles, and barriers that test our abilities, our persistence, and our faith.

Life itself is one long test, which means some parts are bound to be hard. Viewing life as an ongoing exam may help you keep your sanity, your perspective, and your faith when troubles come your way. After all, God is the proctor, but he isn't neutral. He even gave you the answer you need to pass with flying colors; that answer is "Jesus."

Experience is a hard teacher because she gives the test first, the lesson afterward.
> -- Former major league pitcher Vernon Law

Life is a test that God wants you to ace.

DAY 83

RUN FOR IT

Read John 20:1-10.

"Peter and the other disciple started for the tomb. Both were running, but the other disciple outran Peter and reached the tomb first" (vv. 3-4).

When you think about Florida athletes who do an inordinate amount of running, basketball players and cross-country runners probably come to mind first. Better think soccer.

Florida's is the most successful soccer program in the SEC with more conference championships than anybody else and a national title in 1998. That success requires an intensity usually associated with higher profile sports as one visit to the soccer practice field attests.

It's hot there. The facility has no shade, and perspiring team members will tell you quite sincerely that it's one of the hottest spots on campus. The heat doesn't slow anybody down, though; it only adds to the challenge of the workouts -- which consist of a lot of running.

"All you do is run," forward Ashlee Elliot said in 2007. Elliot said a typical practice includes running more than three miles -- and in the preseason the team practices three times a day. "People don't think we run as much as other teams, but we do."

A California native, Elliot remembers that she "couldn't even breathe on the first day I was here." The players run so much they sometimes wear heart monitors to avoid problems with heat stroke.

All that running, though, gives the Florida soccer players a definite advantage because many of their home games are played in the early afternoon. "Other teams . . . are in for a real treat when they see how hot it is here," junior Ameera Abdullah said.

And in that heat the Gator soccer team runs and runs -- to victory.

Hit the ground running -- every morning that's what you do as you leave the house and re-enter the rat race. You run errands, you run though a presentation; you give someone a run for his money; you always want to be in the running and never run-of-the-mill.

You're always running toward something, such as your goals, or away from something, such as your past. Many of us spend much of our lives foolhardily attempting to run away from God, the purposes he has for us, and the blessings he is waiting to give us. No matter how hard or how far you run, though, you can never outrun yourself or God. God keeps pace with you, calling you in the short run to take care of the long run by falling to your knees and running for your life -- to Jesus -- just as Peter and the other disciple ran that first Easter morning.

On your knees, you run all the way to glory.

A lot of people run a race to see who's the fastest. I run to see who has the most guts.
>   -- All-American long-distance runner Steve Prefontaine

You can run to eternity by going to your knees.

DAY 84

HEAD GAMES

Read 1 Peter 1:3-16.

"Prepare your minds for action" (v. 13).

They were strong enough and talented enough physically, but did they have what it took between the ears? Were the Gators of 2006 tough enough mentally to stand tall when everything was falling apart?

They got the answer on Sept. 16 in Knoxville. Everything was going wrong for the Gators, and they appeared headed for yet another heartache on the road. They trailed 10-7 in the second quarter when freshman Brandon James waltzed his way through the Vols for an 84-yard punt return, but the touchdown was called back. Right before the half ended, the Gators missed a field goal. Then Tennessee came out and scored early in the third quarter: 17-7.

Time to fold, right? But this team -- as the rest of the season would attest -- was tough, mentally *and* physically.

With 1:16 left in the third quarter, quarterback Chris Leak hit Dallas Baker with a four-yard toss to make it 17-14. Another Tennessee field goal upped the lead to 20-14 in the fourth, but the Vols were through scoring for the day. The Gators weren't. With 6:30 to play, Leak and Baker hooked up again, this time on a 21-yard pass play. Florida led 21-20.

Tennessee had one last chance to save itself, but safety Reggie

Nelson intercepted a pass and the Vols never saw the ball again. On third and six from the Gator 28, tailback Deshawn Wynn picked up the first down. Game over. Coach Urban Mayer called the win "one of the finest team efforts I've ever seen."

Tough physically *and* mentally, the Gators had persevered.

Once upon a time, survival required mere brute strength, but persevering in American society today generally necessitates mental strength rather than physical prowess.

Your job, your family, your finances -- they all demand mental toughness from you by placing stress upon you to perform. Stress is a fact of life, though it isn't all bad as we are often led to believe. Stress can lead you to function at your best. Rather than buckling under it, you stand up, make constant decisions, and keep going.

So it is with your faith life. "Too blessed to be stressed" sounds nice, but followers of Jesus Christ know all about stress. Society screams compromise; your children whine about being cool; your company ignores ethics. But you don't fold beneath the stress; you keep your mind on Christ and the way he said to live because you are tough mentally, strengthened by your faith.

After all, you have God's word and God's grace for relief and support.

You can recognize talent, but it's a bit harder to recognize mental toughness.
— Gator booster Fernando Storch

Toughened mentally by your faith in Christ,
you live out what you believe, and you persevere.

DAY 85

AN AMERICAN HERO

Read 1 Samuel 16:1-13.

"Do not consider his appearance or his height, for . . . the Lord does not look at the things man looks at. . . . The Lord looks at the heart" (v. 7).

Forrest "Fergie" Ferguson is a Florida football legend, but he is also an American hero.

Ferguson was a three-year starter at end on both offense and defense who was All-America in 1941. His school receiving records stood until the pro-style passing era of modern times. Since 1954, the university has presented the Ferguson Award in his memory to honor "the senior football player who displays outstanding leadership, character and courage."

In 1939 against Boston College, Ferguson provided veteran UF broadcaster Otis Boggs, who did the play-by-play on radio for 403 Florida games from 1939-'82, "the greatest performance I was ever associated with. . . . It was just superb."

BC was a four-touchdown favorite, but Florida scored early to lead 7-0. Eight times in the last three quarters, the Eagles moved inside the Gator 15, and each time the Ferguson-led defense repelled them.

Finally, with three minutes left to play, the Eagles appeared to save themselves when they returned a Gator punt to the 15. On first down, Ferguson fought off two blockers and made the tackle at the line of scrimmage. After an incomplete pass on second down, a double-teamed Ferguson stopped a BC run at the twelve. He then bulldozed past yet another double-team to sack the BC quarterback on fourth down and preserve one of Florida's greatest victories ever. In all, Ferguson had five sacks and six touchdown-saving tackles.

But Ferguson showed his mettle on another battlefield. As a second lieutenant in 1944, he was severely wounded in the invasion of Normandy. He won the Distinguished Service Cross for heroism under fire and died of his wounds ten years later.

A hero is commonly thought of as someone who performs brave and dangerous feats that save or protect someone's life – as Forrest Ferguson did. You figure that excludes you.

But ask your son about that when you show him how to bait a hook, or your daughter when you show up for her dance recital. Look into the eyes of those Little Leaguers you help coach.

Ask God about heroism when you're steady in your faith. For God, a hero is a person with the heart of a servant. And if a hero is a servant who acts to save other's lives, then the greatest hero of all is Jesus Christ.

God seeks heroes today, those who will proclaim the name of their hero – Jesus – proudly and boldly, no matter how others may scoff or ridicule. God knows a hero when he sees him -- by how he acts and also by what's in his heart.

Heroes and cowards feel exactly the same fear; heroes just act differently.
– Late boxing trainer Cus D'Amato

God's heroes are those who remain steady
in their faith while serving others.

DAY 86

SCHOOL DAYS

Read Matthew 13:10-17.

"The knowledge of the secrets of the kingdom of heaven has been given to you" (v. 11).

The Gators had a secret weapon in their national championship game against UCLA on April 3, 2006: They had gone to school.

Florida won its first-ever NCAA basketball championship with a 73-57 drumming of the Bruins. The Gators played great offensively with four players -- Joakim Noah, Lee Humphrey, Al Horford, and Corey Brewer -- scoring in double digits. They won the game, though, in large part because of their defense. Sophomore forward Corey Brewer pointed that out when he said, "People were talking . . . about UCLA's defense. No one talked about our defense. We kind of took that personally."

Florida stifled the helpless Bruins. They shot only 36.1 percent for the game and 17.6 percent from three-point range. The Gators blocked ten shots and snatched seven steals.

It was almost as if the Gators knew what the Bruins were going to do before they did it. They did.

During UCLA's semifinal win over LSU, assistant coach Donnie Jones noticed that a Bruin assistant relayed the plays to the players on the court by holding up cards that had the plays on them, such as "Nevada" or "14-X."

So the Gator coaches knew something valuable about their opponents. The coaches then prepared their players for what

GATORS

they would do in response. As a result, every time those cards went up against Florida, Jones quickly yelled instructions to his defenders.

Armed with their inside information, the Gators knew what was coming and were ready for it. The Gators truly graduated at the head of their class: national champions.

We can never know too much. We once thought our formal education ended when we entered the workplace, but now we have constant training sessions, conferences, and seminars to keep us current whether our expertise is in auto mechanics or medicine. Many areas require graduate degrees now as we scramble to stay abreast of new discoveries and information. And still we never know it all. We are constantly going back to school.

Nowhere, however, is the paucity of our knowledge more stark than it is when we consider God. We will never know even a fraction of all there is to apprehend about the creator of the universe – with one important exception. God has revealed all we need to know about the kingdom of heaven to ensure our salvation. He has opened to us great and eternal secrets.

All we need to know about getting into Heaven is right there in the Bible. With God, ignorance is no excuse and knowledge is salvation.

I've never known a day when I didn't learn something new about this game.

— *Connie Mack on baseball*

When it comes to our salvation, we can indeed know it all; God has revealed everything to us we need to know.

DAY 87

LANGUAGE BARRIER

Read Acts 2:1-21.

"Divided tongues, as of fire, appeared among them, and a tongue rested on each of them. All of them were filled with the Holy Spirit and began to speak in other languages, as the Spirit gave them ability" (vv. 3-4 NRSV).

Language problems once contributed to Florida's own version of a "Cuban Crisis" that resulted in the Gator head football coach being thrown in jail.

The 1912 squad was 4-2-1, including a 10-6 win over South Carolina and wins over the College of Charleston and Stetson, when it made the most unique trip in Florida football history. The team hopped aboard a boat and went to Havana to play two Cuban all-star teams.

On Christmas Day, Florida won the first game easily 27-0 with things pretty much going off without a hitch. The second game, on Dec. 30, was another matter entirely.

The referees put a particularly Cuban spin onto the interpretation of the rules, and Florida coach G.E. Pyle didn't appreciate it. His English and the refs' Spanish didn't help matters very much either. After one particularly flagrant violation of the rules by the Spanish team, Pyle protested and demanded the prescribed 15-yard penalty. To Pyle's dismay, the ref offered a bargain: five yards or none. Pyle refused to deal, and the official declared the game forfeited.

A near-riot broke out, and Cuban police arrested Pyle. He had part of a trial before it was postponed, and during the recess, he hopped aboard a ship and made for home. The 0-0 tie is not included in the Florida record books though the 27-0 win is.

As the Gators' trip to Cuba illustrates, our games don't always translate across national and cultural boundaries. Language, though, is what usually erects a barrier to understanding. Recall your overseas vacation or your call to a tech support number when you got someone who spoke English but didn't understand it. Talking loud and waving your hands doesn't facilitate communication; it just makes you look weird.

Like many other aspects of life, faith has its jargon that can sometimes hinder understanding. Sanctification, justification, salvation, Advent, Communion with its symbolism of eating flesh and drinking blood – these and many other words have specific meanings to Christians that may be incomprehensible, confusing, and downright daunting to the newcomer or the seeker.

But the heart of Christianity's message centers on words that require no explanation: words such as hope, joy, love, purpose, and community. Their meanings are universal because people the world over seek them in their lives. Nobody speaks that language better than Jesus.

Kindness is the universal language that all people understand.
-- Legendary Florida A&M coach Jake Gaither

Jesus speaks across all language barriers
because his message of hope and meaning
resounds with people everywhere.

DAY 88

WHO, ME?

Read Judges 6:11-23.

"'But Lord,' Gideon asked, 'how can I save Israel? My clan is the weakest in Manasseh, and I am the least in my family'" (v. 15).

You could hear a pin drop."

The silence was deafening in the Florida football locker room on Nov. 3, 1973, just minutes before the kickoff against Auburn. Sophomore Don Gaffney had just been told he was starting the game at quarterback -- his first start.

Gaffney would letter three times, earn Second-Team All-SEC honors in 1975, and be inducted into the Florida-Georgia Hall of Fame. But all that was ahead of Gaffney that November day when Coach Doug Dickey surprised him by walking up, handing him a football, and declaring, "Don, you got it."

Gaffney had been a little suspicious that he might play some. He had called his dad the night before and told him he had been "getting a strange feeling" because he was "getting too many snaps in practice." The coaches had used an off-week to switch to the veer offense to take advantage of Gaffney's speed and shiftiness. Offensive Coordinator Jimmy Dunn "kept saying things to me about making sure I got my hands underneath center and the crowd noise, things he had never said before."

Despite Gaffney's suspicions and his heads-up to his dad, he went through warm-ups as usual. "Nothing was said," and he had little conviction that he'd be starting. Then Dickey dropped the bombshell.

Running back Nat Moore walked over to the surprised sophomore and offered his support: "Gaff, go play your game. This is your time." Defensive back Wayne Fields was in Gaffney's corner. "It's about time," he said. "This is what we've been waiting for."

And how did Gaffney do? He completed 6-of-10 passes including one for a touchdown as Florida upset Auburn 12-8.

You probably know exactly how Don Gaffney felt; you've experienced that sinking "who, me?" feeling.

How about that time the teacher called on you when you hadn't done a lick of homework? Or the night the hypnotist pulled you out of a room full of folks to be his guinea pig? You've had the wide-eyed look and the turmoil in your midsection when you were suddenly singled out and found yourself in a situation you neither sought nor were prepared for.

You may feel the same way Gideon did about being called to serve God in some way, quailing at the very notion of being audacious enough to teach Sunday school, lead a small group study, or coordinate a high school prayer club. After all, who's worthy enough to do anything like that?

The truth is that nobody is – but that doesn't seem to matter to God. And it's his opinion, not yours, that counts.

Surprise me.
> *-- Yogi Berra on where his wife should have him buried*

You're right in that no one is worthy to serve God, but the problem is that doesn't matter to God.

DAY 89

DYNASTY

Read 2 Samuel 7:8-17.

"Your house and your kingdom will endure forever before me; your throne will be established forever" (v. 16).

In the history of SEC competition, the Florida volleyball team stands alone with a dynasty the likes of which defies comprehension in the super-competitive league.

With a defeat of South Carolina on Nov. 26, 2008, the Gator volleyball team won its eighteenth straight SEC championship, which set the record for the most consecutive SEC titles ever in any sport. Florida had been tied with the Arkansas men's cross-country team, but their streak came to an end at 17 in 2008.

The Gator dominance in volleyball began when Coach Mary Wise arrived in Gainesville in 1991 from Kentucky and promptly "propelled a once lackluster program into the epitome of excellence." The Gators won the league title her first year -- and the dynasty began. So dominant have the Gators been that they went more than 10 seasons from 1994-2004 without losing a regular-season SEC match. During the 2003 season, the Gators won 105 straight games, smashing the previous NCAA record by 36 games.

The record against SEC opponents is almost embarrassing. Since Wise arrived and through the 2008 season, the Florida league record looks like this: Alabama 28-0, Arkansas 26-2, Auburn 26-0, Georgia 44-1, Kentucky 39-0, LSU 37-3, Ole Miss 28-0, Miss. State

25-0, South Carolina, 35-2, and Tennessee 34-4. (Vanderbilt did not field a team.)

The Florida volleyball team has established a dynasty that has never been or is never likely to be equaled in SEC history. And it's still rolling on.

Inevitably, someone will snap the Gators' streak of volleyball conference championships. History teaches us that kingdoms, empires, countries, and even sports programs rise and fall. Dynasties end as events and circumstances conspire and align to snap all winning streaks.

Your life is like that; you win some and lose some. You get a promotion on Monday and your son gets arrested on Friday. You breeze through your annual physical but your dog dies. You finally line up a date with that cutie next door and get sent out of town on business.

Only one dynasty will never end because it is based upon an everlasting promise from God. God promised David the king an enduring line in the appearance of one who would establish God's kingdom forever. That one is Jesus Christ, the reigning king of God's eternal and unending dynasty.

The only way to lose out on that one is to stand on the sidelines and not get in the game.

Dynasties, streaks, and careers all come to an end eventually.
                                                    -- ESPN's Mr. Clean

**All dynasties and win streaks end except the one
God established with Jesus as its king;
this one never loses and never will.**

DAY 90

A SECOND CHANCE

Read John 7:53–8:11.

"'Then neither do I condemn you,' Jesus declared. 'Go now and leave your life of sin'" (v. 8:11).

Football is an unforgiving game; rarely does it give a team a second chance. The Gators got one, though, in 1996.

Florida's national championship aspirations had apparently been left in Tallahassee after a 24-21 loss to FSU in the season's last regular-season game. But on Dec. 7, Texas upset Nebraska in the Big 12 title game to derail the expected Cornhusker-FSU match-up in the Sugar Bowl.

Pumped up by the Texas win, the Gators took care of business with a 45-30 pasting of Alabama for their fourth straight SEC title. The 45 points were the most ever scored in an SEC Championship Game and the most Alabama had given up in 26 years. Now ranked no. 3, Florida had a second chance at the national title.

Two things had to happen, though: a win over top-ranked FSU in a rematch in the Sugar Bowl and a loss by second-ranked Arizona State to fifth-ranked Ohio State in the Rose Bowl.

Linebacker James Bates recalled that as the Gators got off the buses in Louisiana they "all ran to our rooms real quick" to watch the remainder of the Rose Bowl. With only 19 seconds left, the Buckeyes scored to win it, and "the orange-and-blue celebration started." "We were running around the hotel courtyard. Gators were going crazy," Bates said about the revelry.

One more item of business remained. Their fate now back in their own hands, the Gators exploded for four straight touchdowns in the last half to embarrass FSU 52-20, the largest margin of victory against the No. one-ranked team in bowl history.

Presented with a rare second chance by what Danny Wuerffel called "an unbelievable set of circumstances," the Gators made the most of their gift -- and were national champions.

"If I just had a second chance, I know I could make it work out." Ever said that? If only you could go back and tell your dad one last time you love him, take that job you passed up rather than relocate, or marry someone else. If only you had a second chance, a mulligan.

As the story of Jesus' encounter with the adulterous woman illustrates, with God you always get a second chance. No matter how many mistakes you make, God will never give up on you. Nothing you can do puts you beyond God's saving power. You always have a second chance because with God your future is not determined by your past or who you used to be. It is determined by your relationship with God through Jesus Christ.

God is ready and willing to give you a second chance – or a third chance or a fourth chance – if you will give him a chance.

God gave us a mulligan.
-- Steve Spurrier after the improbable events that led to Florida's playing in the 1996 national championship game

You get a second chance with God if you will give him a chance.

NOTES
(Devotional Day Number)

1 In 1899, student pressure . . . agree to a football team.: Arthur Cobb, *Go Gators!* (Pensacola: Sunshine Publishing Co., 1966) p. 8.

1 An engineering teacher, . . . to be the head coach.: Marty Cohen, *Gator Tales* (Wichita, Kansas: The Wichita Eagle and Beacon Publishing Co., 1995), p. 7.

1 The pastor of the Lake City . . . never played a game.: Cobb, p. 8.

1 More than 2,000 "wildly excited" . . . there were no seats.: Cobb, p. 9.

1 FAC's best chance to score . . . and Stetson held.: Cobb, p. 9.

1 FAC played Stetson again in 1902 . . . played until 1906: Cohen, p. 7.

2 The Wall of Florida . . . five of the 2007 Gator soccer team's.: Danny Klein, "Tough Defense Leads UF Soccer," *The Independent Florida Alligator*, Sept. 20, 2007, http://www.alligator.org/articles/2007/09/20/sports/other_gator?sports_asoccer.txt, Jan. 9, 2008.

2 "Offense may win games, but defense wins championships.": Klein, "Tough Defense."

2 'We have a lot of big girls . . . knock some people down.": Klein, "Tough Defense."

3 "When Kerwin came into the huddle . . . magic words to us,": Peter Kerasotis, *Stadium Stories: Florida Gators* (Guilford, CN: The Globe Pequot Press, 2005), p. 92.

3 "swiftly and methodically": Kerasotis, p. 92.

3 "limped toward the goal line . . . barely squeezed in": Kerasotis, p. 92.

4 The *Gainesville Sun* said . . . 6-0 at the break.: Cobb, p. 164.

4 At halftime, Maj. James A. Van Fleet . . . bit of national prominence.: Cobb, p. 165.

5 On Nov. 8, 1994 . . . for your Florida Gators!": Brandon Zimmerman, "UF Volleyball's Hampton Lives out Her Dream," *The Gainesville Sun*, Nov. 18, 2007, http://www.gatorsports.com/article/2007/1118/NEWS/71118002, Nov. 26, 2007.

5 "Not a lot of people . . . This is really cool.": Zimmerman, "UF Volleyball's Hampton."

6 quarterback Danny Wuerffel faked an injury . . . two-yard touchdown pass from Wuerffel to Doering.: Cohen, pp. 140-41.

7 Florida coach Charlie Strong . . . and Strong relented.: Robbie Andreu, "Spurrier's Return a Losing One," *A Year for the Gators* (Gainesville: The Gainesville Sun, 2007), p. 85.

7 "Looking back on Florida's . . . effort by a great performer.": Robbie Andreu, "Florida's Blockbuster Play," *The Gainesville Sun*, Nov. 6, 2007, http:www.gainesvillesun.com/article/20071106/NEWS/711060308, Jan. 1, 2008.

7 "We already knew we were going to block it,": Andreu, "Florida's Blockbuster Play."

7 whom Strong originally wanted in the game.: Andreu, "Spurrier's

Return," p. 80.

7   "We already knew we were going to get the push up front.": Andreu, "Florida's Blockbuster Play."

7   During the timeout before . . . a chance to block the kick.: Andreu, "Spurrier's Return," p. 85.

7   "That was the biggest play I've ever made,": Andreu, "Spurrier's Return," p. 85.

8   While Florida doesn't include . . . in 1904 in Macon, Ga.: Kerasotis, pp. 2-3.

8   Florida officials argue . . . in Gainesville until 1906.: Kerasotis, p. 2.

8   The game was played in Jacksonville . . . folks could attend the game.: Kerasotis, p. 3.

8   the *Florida Times-Union* . . . football in this city.": Kerasotis, p. 4.

9   Yun was believed to be . . . to and from campus every day.: Brandon Zimmerman, "15-Year-Old Takes on UF, Golf," *The Gainesville Sun*, Feb. 11, 2008, http://www.gainesville.com/article/20080211/NEWS/802110319, May 7, 2008.

10   "The Swamp is where Gators live,": Kerasotis, p. 114.

10   Earl "Dummy" Taylor played . . . to ever wear a shoe.": Cobb, p. 11.

10   "Cannonball" Clyde Crabtree, who passed with either hand effortlessly.: Cohen, p. 23.

10   Art "Stump" Wright . . . in the infirmary.: Cohen, p. 49.

10   Jimmy "Mighty Mite" Dunn . . . TD to beat Georgia.: Cohen, p. 55.

11   He knew how good his senior . . . college football had ever known.": Kerasotis, p. 22.

11   Not a single Florida game . . . voters from the South.: Kerasotis, p. 24.

11   Carlson even got the governor . . . plays from the 1966 season.: Kerasotis, pp. 24-5.

11   "To win the Heisman Trophy . . . without winning Californis,": Kerasotis, p. 25.

12   Brown's special night was driven . . . so it's up to me.": Ian Thomsen, "Swamped," *Sports Illustrated*, Sept. 27, 1999, http://vault.sportsillustrated.cnn.com/vault/article/magazine/MAG1017130/index.htm, May 5, 2008.

13   Florida grad Ryan Weinstein found himself . . . pre-game practices he never missed.: Amy Reinink, "Gators Go for Glory," *The Gainesville Sun*, March 31, 2007, http://www.gainesville.com/article/20070331/LO-CAL/703310355, May 12, 2008.

14   They gather faithfully . . . you still have to eat it.": Brandon Zimmerman, "Breakfast Club Helps UF Players Pack Pounds," *The Gainesville Sun*, Sept. 25, 2007, http://www.gainesvillesun.com/article/20070925/NEWS/709250316, Jan. 1, 2008.

15   "the most sensational and . . . their days of Camelot.": Kerasotis, p. 107.

15   "unprecedented success and . . . the hint of cheating.": Kerasotis, p. 106.

15   "What Florida needed . . . instill those in the team.: Kerasotis, p. 109.

15   We had the attitude . . . no matter what happens.": Kerasotis, p. 110.

15   "He was telling us . . . he made you believe.": Kerasotis, p. 109.

16   "filled with an overabundance . . . could easily be shattered." Cobb, p. 102.

16   "Mark this . . . foundation under Florida football.": Fred Pettijohn, *Fort Lauderdale News*, quoted in Cobb, p. 102.

16   "push[ed] the Gators from the bottom into the upper division": Cohen, p. 42.

16   "bold steps aimed at . . . top of the SEC.": Cohen, p. 42.

16   "made the entire sports program go.": Cohen, p. 48.

16   "We do not choose whether . . . on which we will stand.": R. Alan Culpepper, "The Gospel of Luke," *The New Interpreter's Bible*, Vol. IX (Nashville, TN: Abingdon Press, 1995), p. 153.

16   Jesus Christ is the rock upon which I stand.: Danny Wuerffel with Mike Bianchi, *Tales from the Gator Swamp* (Champaign, IL: Sports Publishing L.L.C., 2006), p. 149.

17   "a program with the potential . . . among the nation's elite.": "Rhonda Faehn, Head Coach," *Florida Gymnastics 2008*, http://www.gatorzone.com/gymnastics/media/2008/pdf/staff/faehn.pdf, p. 8, June 28, 2008.

17   She was still in . . . have asked for more.": Brandon Zimmerman, "Faehn Returns with Gators No. 1," *The Gainesville Sun*, Jan. 15, 2008, http://www.gainesville.com/article/20080115/NEWS/212524708, May 7, 2008.

18   Mickey Marotti's offseason conditioning . . . especially the workouts.": Robbie Andreu, "UF Strength Coach Marotti Teaches Players Chemistry," *The Gainesville Sun*, June 7, 2008, http://www.gainesville.com/article/20080607/NEWS/599210388, June 26, 2008.

19   It is getting so you can't figure football no more.": Cobb, p. 184.

19   On Nov. 27, 1965, Florida . . . to finish the Noles.: Cobb, pp. 184-85.

19   "It was certainly the finest victory of my career,": Cobb, p. 185.

19   It's amazing. Some of the greatest . . . to be a Christian man.: Bettinger, p. 121.

20   All-American defensive end . . . "Right, right.": Wilton Sharpe, *Gators Glory* (Nashville, TN: Cumberland House, 2007), p. 140.

20   The season before they had . . . "There's Just No Way.": Cohen, p. 78.

20   On the first play . . . for a 70-yard touchdown,: Cohen, p. 78-79.

20   thousands of Gator fans were streaming . . . this incredible upset.": Cohen, p. 79.

21   In Florida's first-round . . . and wanted to play.": Kevin Brockway, "#13 Joakim Noah," *Florida Gators: 2006 NCAA Champions* (Gainesville: *The Gainesville Sun*, 2006), p. 28.

21   the morning after the 2005-06 season . . . last ones to leave.": Brockway, "#13 Joakim Noah, p. 28.

21   The coaches "just told me to keep working,": Brockway, "#13 Joakim Noah," p. 28.

22   "a little guy among the giants,": Pat Dooley, "Higgins Is Florida's 'Rudy,'" *A Year for the Gators* (Gainesville: The Gainesville Sun, 2007), p. 94.

22   He was Tim Higgins . . . everything we asked him to do,": Dooley, "Higgins Is Florida's 'Rudy,'" p. 93.

22   "There were times when . . . wondered why I was here.": Dooley, "Higgins Is Florida's 'Rudy,'" p. 94.

22   the fans began to chant . . . "So I gave them Higgins.": Dooley, "Higgins Is Florida's 'Rudy,'" p. 93.

22   He sent Higgins in at . . . stopped for no gain,": Dooley, "Higgins Is Florida's 'Rudy,'" p. 94.

23   "A swamp is hot and sticky and can be dangerous.": Sharpe, p. 190.

23   "There is no better place than 'The Swamp,'": *Florida 2007 Guide*, p. 46, http://www.gatorzone.com/football/media/2007/pdf/46/pdf.

23   With an original capacity of 21,769,: *Florida 2007 Guide*, p. 46.

23   Florida Field was constructed . . . More than 20,000 fans: Cohen, p. 28.

23   The first of many expansions . . . at Florida Field in 1989,: *Florida 2007 Guide*, p. 46.

23   further expansions raised the capacity to more than 90,000.: *Florida 2007 Guide*, p. 47.

24   The whirlwind of activities . . . the man of the hour.": Wuerffel, p. 150.

24   His mom, who, Wuerffel said, . . . swayed and sang along.": Wuerffel, p. 151.

24   A smaller banquet . . . good music and questionable dancing.": Wuerffel, p. 149.

24   Included in that dancing was . . . a tremendous play-caller.": Wuerffel, p. 150.

25   He told FSU Coach . . . my one and only offers.": Pat Dooley, *Game of My Life:* (Champaign, IL: Sports Publishing L.L.C., 2007), p. 240.

26   With only four minutes . . . in the last 8:42.: "No Panic, Gators Just Come up Clutch," *The Gainesville Sun*, March 23, 2007, http://www.gainesvillecom/article/20070323/COLUMNISTS/70323035, May 12, 2008.

27   "Awash in color and noise.": Wuerffel, p. 47.

27   "one of the most surreal things . . . and above you.": Wuerffel, p. 47.

27   "the greatest environment in all of college football.": Wuerffel, p. 48.

27   the fabled Gator war cry . . . The battle cry was born.: Cobb, pp. 2-3.

27   The Swamp rocked like never before . . . in the parking lot.": Sharpe, p. 187.

28   "for an hour after the loss . . . without saying a word.": Austin Murphy, "Tim Tebow," *Sports Illustrated Presents Florida Gators*, Jan. 14, 2009, p. 55.

28   "You have never seen any player . . . a tear for the ages.": Murphy, p. 56.

29   a performance that inspired . . . called "Hunsinger the Humdinger.": Cobb, p. 54.

29   If Hunsinger liked anything . . . first half against Georgia.: Cobb, p. 2.

29   Hearin made good . . . named his new bird dog "Blocker.": Cobb, p. 2.

30   "It was a frustrating game . . . field goal kicker Wayne Barfield: Kerasotis, p. 42.

30   Spurrier went over to . . . a shot at this one.": Kerasotis, p. 43.

30   Graves agreed without hesitating . . . a field goal to beat Auburn.": Kerasotis, p. 42.

30   "No doubt," . . . middle of the goalposts.": Kerasotis, p. 43.

30   When Spurrier trotted onto the field . . . he will make it.": Kerasotis, p. 43.

31   The deadline Tebow had . . . no better place than right here.": Robbie Andreu, "Team Tebow," *The Gainesville Sun*, Dec. 9, 2007, http://www.gainesvillesun.com/article/20071210/NEWS/71209024, Jan. 1, 2008.

32   the Hula Bowl invited . . . so I accepted.": Dooley, *Game of My Life*, p. 61.

33   The University Athletic Association . . . in time for the ceremony.: Kevin Brockway, "Thanks for the Memories," *The Gainesville Sun*, April 7, 2007, http://www.gainesville.com/article/20070407/SUN-FRONT/704070340, May 8, 2008.

33   one-by-two foot chunks . . . floor one last time.: Brockway, "Thanks for the Memories."

34   "I would probably have said . . . and bigger and stronger.": Dooley, *Game of My Life*, p. 88.

34   With a little urging from . . . team in the spring.: Dooley, *Game of My Life*, pp. 88-89.

34   But when Dunn put on . . . the football team for long.": Dooley, *Game of My Life*, p. 89.

34   except for the time . . . to put some weight on him.: Dooley, *Game of My Life*, p. 90.

35   "for more than 50 years . . . "a scoring juggernaut.": Cohen, p. 22.

35   tops in the nation: Cohen, p. 23.

35   who could pass with either hand: Cohen, p. 23.

35   "perfect conditions to slow down the potent Gators.": Cohen, p. 23.

35   An irate Bachman accused . . . mud was left behind.: Al Browning, *Chomp 'Em Gators* (Sterett, Al.: Colonial BancGroup, 2001), p. 203.

36   In the summer of 2007 . . . and ready to go.": "Break from Game Beneficial for UF's McGinnis," *The Gainesville Sun*, Oct. 10, 2007, http://www.gainesville.com/article/20071010/NEWS/71010006, May 8, 2008.

37   He required players to do 42 reps at each station.: Andy Staples, "Taking the Bite out of the Dawgs," *Sports Illustrated Presents Florida Gators*, Jan. 14, 2009, p. 27.

37   Marotti also added sets . . . after 2007's first touchdown.: Staples.

37   That wasn't right. . . . the mind of our football team: Staples.

38   in the fall of 1907 . . . at the University of Virginia.: Cohen, p. 25.

38   So Miller contacted the outfit . . . a photo of an alligator.: Cohen, p. 25.

38   and traced it.: Cobb, p. 12.

38 By the fall of 1908 . . . teams were the "Alligators,": Cohen, p. 25.

38 some pompous sportswriters sometimes . . . a group of reptiles.: Cohen, p. 7.

38 "I had no idea it would stick or even be popular with the student body.: Cohen, p. 25.

39 One scout pegged him . . . player in the country.: Kerasotis, p. 90.

39 "We needed something to . . . that run did it.": Kerasotis, p. 93.

39 "If you want to get through . . . you'll get through it,": Kerasotis, p. 96.

39 In football, you can get on that field . . . heart and soul in it.": Sharpe, p. 52.

40 "a peon compared to those guys,": Pat Dooley, "#2 Corey Brewer, " *Florida Gators: 2006 NCAA Champions* (Gainesville: *The Gainesville Sun*, 2006), p. 100.

40 He raised tobacco and soybeans . . . that was a great lesson,": Dooley, "#2 Corey Brewer," p. 100.

40 "My daddy's not famous . . . all his life.": Dooley, "#2 Corey Brewer," p. 101.

40 "makes him famous enough.": Dooley, "#2 Corey Brewer, p. 101.

41 when Spurrier arrived in Gainesville . . . moving the game to home-and-home.: Kerasotis, pp. 107-08.

42 not until 1914 did Pug Hamilton . . . the band director's hand.: "The Pride of the Sunshine," *Wikipedia, the free encyclopedia*, http://en.wikipedia.orga/wiki/The_Pride_of_the_Sunshine, June 26, 2008.

43 On Tuesday before the game . . . uncle of mine started booing.": Dooley, *Game of My Life*, p. 45.

43 "I'm taking the last snap." He did,: Dooley, *Game of My Life*, p. 47.

43 He alternated all three of them.: Dooley, *Game of My Life*, p. 47.

43 Willie Jackson was probably . . . who came out of nowhere.: Sharpe, p. 39.

44 "When you watch the replays, . . . Danny Wuerffel got back up. Kerasotis, p. 130.

44 Many Heisman voters . . . required a special quarterback.: Kerasotis, p. 131.

45 In August 2005, Hurricane . . . "It's home.": Brandon Zimmerman, "Thompson Had Long Journey Home," *The Gainesville Sun*, Jan. 30, 2008, http://www.gatorsports.com/article/20080130/NEWS/4456524/1016, Jan. 31, 2008.

46 he wasn't particularly fast . . . rain pelted the passengers.: Dooley, *Game of My Life*, p. 50.

46 When he landed in Jacksonville . . . That sold me.": Dooley, *Game of My Life*, p. 51.

47 "Wow! Did I just . . . she did that tonight.": Brandon Zimmerman, "Sinclair Perfect in Florida's Win," *The Gainesville Sun*, March 3, 2007, http://www.gainesville.com/article/20070303/GATORS18/703030313, May 14, 2008.

47 Guise, who was part of . . . girls are it looks easy.":

Zimmerman, "Sinclair Perfect in Florida's Win."

48 "It's an incredible advantage.": *Florida 2007 Guide*, p. 50.

48 Matthew Waxman . . . has crossed your mind.": *Florida 2007 Guide*, p. 50.

48 "Both sides of the stadium . . . on top of the action.": *Florida 2007 Guide*, p. 50.

48 Fans watched the games . . . along the sidelines.: Sharpe, p. 184.

48 From 1908 through . . . an incredible 25-0-1 record.: Cohen, p. 12.

49 "I know that coach . . . We just didn't make the play.".: Pat Dooley, "Fake Punt Sunk [sic] Rebels' Chances," *The Gainesville Sun*, Sept. 22, 2007, http://www.gainesville.com/article/20070922/NEWS/70922013, May 8, 2008.

50 Spurrier admitted that they didn't play very well.: Kerasotis, p. 47.

50 "We were at midfield with . . . "That's terrible," Spurrier retorted.": Kerasotis, p. 47.

50 When you are doing . . . your time is going to come.: Sharpe, p. 52.

51 But they got help from . . . "sense of youthful wonder".: Grant Wahl, "The Gators Again," *Sports Illustrated*, April 9, 2007, http://vault.sports-illustrated.cnn.com/vault/article/magazine/MAG1104568/2/index.htm, May 5, 2008.

52 with orders to move . . . the upper echelons of the SEC.: Cohen, p. 42.

52 "slow-talking, somewhat gruff . . . in superior health.": Cohen, p. 42.

52 on Dec. 2, 1959, Cohen, p. 59.

52 recruiting 26 players whom . . . were not more appreciated.: Cohen, p. 59.

52 Don't go to your grave with a life unused.: Bettinger, p. 76.

53 "laid the groundwork for all the bright and wonderful things": Kerasotis, p. 52.

53 "There wasn't room for anything . . . obsession to a fault.": Frank Litsky, "Charley Pell Is Dead at 60; Ousted as Florida Coach," *The New York Times*, May 31, 2001, http://query.nytimes.com/gst/fullpage.html, June 26, 2008.

53 "belligerent, flagrant, and deliberate.": Kerasotis, p. 61.

53 "among the most serious . . . by the NCAA.": Kerasotis, p. 64.

53 "Charley Pell had the most . . . next to Steve Spurrier.": Kerasotis, p. 65.

53 "a fractured fan base . . . even embarrassingly – substandard.": Kerasotis, p. 54.

54 "the biggest upset of the Coach Spurrier era.": Wuerffel, p. 23.

54 Prior to the game, . . . receiver named Chris Doering.: Kerasotis, p. 126.

54 Spurrier sent four receivers wide, . . . I really can't!": Kerasotis, p. 128.

55 The Gators sat on top . . . win for our ball club.".: Brandon Zimmerman, "UF Walks off with Monster Rally," *The Gainesville Sun*, April 7, 2007, http://www.gainesville.com/article/20070407/GATORS04/70407012, May 8, 2008.

GATORS

56   "Tight end was the world . . . my first dream.": Kerasotis, p. 70.

56   Coach Charley Pell told Marshall he could play tight end at Florida,: Kerasotis, p. 71.

56   "We need you on defense. play at outside linebacker,": Kerasotis, p. 72.

56   "I was like, 'Hey,. . . . to do this anymore.": Kerasotis, pp. 71-72.

56   "A lot of people were . . . So I made the switch.": Kerasotis, p. 72.

57   "you can feel the force of the deafening crowd.": Wuerffel, p. 47.

57   before the Stetson game on . . . yell yourself dumb.": Cohen, p. 9.

57   "talk, think, and dream football. . . . go down to defeat.": Cohen, p. 9.

58   "Nobody gave us a chance," wide receiver Dallas Baker said.: Robbie Andreu, "Gators Make Most of Chances," *A Year for the Gators* (Gainesville: *The Gainesville Sun*, 2007) , p. 114.

58   One newspaper predicted 42-14 Ohio State.: Andreu, "Gators Make Most," p. 120.

58   "There's a team . . . not the Gators.": Andreu, "Gators Make Most," p. 120.

58   "It ain't disrespect . . . it's the truth,": Andreu, "Gators Make Most," p. 123.

58   "Motivation was easy for the last 30 days,": Andreu, "Gators Make Most," p. 120.

58   "I don't want to say . . . exactly what it was.": Andreu, "Gators Make Most," p. 114.

59   Some "experts" . . . fifth in the SEC East.: Kevin Brockway, "Tourney Two-Peat," *Florida Gators: 2006 NCAA Champions* (Gainesville: *The Gainesville Sun*, 2006) p. 68.

59   Coach Billy Donovan called . . . left for the win.: Brockway, "Tourney Two-Peat," p. 73.

60   As their plane coasted along . . . see you in Heaven,": Wuerffel, p. 52.

61   the school didn't have much money . . . a light, unpadded jersey.": Cobb, pp. 8-9.

61   Regulation shoes were too expensive . . . nose guards and shin guards.": Cobb, p. 9.

61   The ball they used was . . . to hold in a hand and pass.: Clyde Bolton, *The Crimson Tide* (Huntsville, AL: The Strode Publishers, 1972), p. 46.

61   threw sticks and rocks at the opposing team: Bolton, *The Crimson Tide*, p. 46.

61   A player might hide the ball under his jersey.: Clyde Bolton, *War Eagle* (Huntsville, AL: The Strode Publishers, 1973), p. 69.

61   Spectators often got in the players' way: Bolton, *War Eagle*, p. 49.

61   threw sticks and rocks at the opposing team: Bolton, *The Crimson Tide*, p. 37.

61   Players dragged ball carriers forward.: Bolton, *War Eagle*, p. 76.

61   Teams decided upon the length of games once they showed up to play.: Bolton, *War Eagle*, p. 80.

61   When dusk threatened, spectators' automobiles were

used to light up the field.: Bolton, *The Crimson Tide*, p. 39.

61 handles were sewn . . . easier to toss.: Bolton, *War Eagle*, p. 76.

62 The Gators moved methodically . . . years of myriad football frustrations.": Cohen, p. 65.

64 His $17,000 salary was more . . . Sooner will be better than later.": Cohen, p. 44.

64 "exploded in an uproar . . . a rare epidemic – football fever.": Cohen, p. 47.

65 He admitted giving . . . because of the rules.": Cohen, p. 124.

65 "belligerent, flagrant, and deliberate" defiance of NCAA rules under Charley Pell: Kerasotis, p. 61.

65 "I'm having a very difficult . . . the removal of the bowl ban,": Cohen, p. 129.

65 None of us wants justice . . . we'd all go to hell.: Bettinger, p. 69.

66 "It was a good year, . . . a pretty good year for the University of Florida.": Dooley, *Game of My Life*, p. 209.

66 The Gators trailed 6-0 . . . run with your pants down.": Dooley, *Game of My Life*, p. 209.

67 As long as you are . . . me to come home.": Pat Dooley, "Waleszonia Reaches Goal Without Her Biggest Supporter," *The Gainesville Sun*, May 28, 2008, http://www.gainesville.com/article/20080528/COLUMNISTS/141001047/1044, June 26, 2008.

67 Waleszonia made the decision . . . feel like I've struggled.": Dooley, "Waleszonia Reaches Goal."

68 "gentle, melodious voice.";: Kerasotis, p. 28.

68 Boggs knew early on . . . had a radio station.: Kerasotis, p. 27.

68 He began his broadcast career . . . Sound effects were put in.": Kerasotis, p. 30.

68 "Most anyone who listened . . . putting down the other team.": Kerasotis, pp. 29-30.

68 "syrupy southern style": Kerasotis, p. 29.

69 She and her husband Bob . . . They named him Timothy.: Suzy A. Richardson, "Coaching Character," *The Gainesville Sun*, Oct. 7, 2007, http://www.gainesville.com/article/20071007/NEWS/710060317, May 8, 2008.

70 The trip to Texas . . . the judge surrendered.": Cobb, p. 4.

70 "The horn actually blew before the ball was placed in play.": Cobb, p. 4.

70 Van Fleet recalled that . . . forgiveness of the good Lord.".: Cobb, p. 5.

70 The rules were a bit . . . from coming between us.: Sharpe, p. 18.

71 "near-flawless.": Robbie Andreu, "Leak Nearly Flawless," *A Year for the Gators* (Gainesville, *The Gainesville Sun*, 2007), p. 18.

71 What Coach Urban Meyer saw . . . Chris Leak's offense now.": Andreu, "Leak Nearly Flawless," p. 18.

71 "I'm real comfortable . . . coaches giving me input.": Andreu, "Leak Nearly Flawless," p. 23.

190

71   ambivalent, vacillating, impulsive . . . "dominant figure" in the birth of the church.: John MacArthur, *Twelve Ordinary Men* (Nashville, TN: W Publishing Group, 2002), p. 39.

72   The Magic were a playoff team . . . the more unhappy he became.: John Feinstein, "After a Change of Heart, Donovan Feels Right at Home," *The Washington Post*, March 8, 2008, http://www.washington-post.com/wpdyn/content/article/2008/03/08, April 26, 2008.

72   "I realized that the one thing . . . was where I belonged.": Feinstein.

73   "All of my Cuban temper came up,": Dooley, *Game of My Life*, p. 4.

73   Alvarez caught only one pass . . . running back and safety.: Dooley, *Game of My Life*, p. 2.

73   the positions for which Florida . . . but he deserved it.": Dooley, *Game of My Life*, p. 4.

73   In 1903, when the game . . . I would not slug him.: Sharpe, p. 17.

74   At Florida's team meeting . . . that does stuff like that.": Brandon Zimmerman, "Emergency Appendectomy Just Not Enough to Stop UF's Mullen," *The Gainesville Sun*, Oct. 2, 2007, http://www.gainesville.com/article/20071002/NEWS/710020325, June 25, 2008.

75   "credited with changing the way . . . offensive and defensive play calling.": "Steve Spurrier," *Wikipedia, the free encyclopedia*, http://en/wikipedia.org/wiki/Steve_Spurrier, June 26, 2008.

75   "It is our job as coaches . . . dedication and a family atmosphere.": Browning, p. 58.

75   I think God made it simple. Just accept Him and believe.: Bettinger, p. 47.

76   they missed ten extra points . . . "never missed a tackle" on defense.: Cobb, p. 23.

76   "hard put to keep from skyrocketing the score.": Cobb, p. 22.

76   The Gators rolled up an incredible . . . Owens scoring four touchdowns.: Cobb, p. 48.

77   The votes came in on Nov. 23, : Kerasotis, p. 46.

77   Spurrier knew he had won the award.: Kerasotis, p. 45.

77   TV cameras weren't even present . . . the winning athlete to keep.: Kerasotis, p. 45.

78   In the April 22, 2007, game . . . to secure the 5-4 win.: Brandon Zimmerman, "Gators Take Their Time to Beat UK," *The Gainesville Sun*, April 22, 2007, http://www.gainesville.com/article/20070422/GA-TORS04/70422008, May 8, 2008.

79   during the week, . . . would be his last.: Dooley, *Game of My Life*, p. 68.

79   "started celebrating like . . . huddled and agreed.: Dooley, *Game of My Life*, p. 70.

79   "We were all wondering . . . celebrating like crazy.": Dooley, *Game of My Life*, p. 70.

80   Florida athletics director Jeremy Foley . . . honored you were our coach.": Brandon Zimmerman, "'We Were Honored You Were Our Coach,'" *The Gainesville Sun*, March 28, 2007,

http://www.gainesville.com/article/20070328/GATORS14/70328007,
May 12, 2008.

80   "The angels now rejoice . . . welcomed him home.": Zimmerman,
"'We Were Honored You Were Our Coach.'"

81   The recruiting letters started . . . showed up at his home.: Dooley,
Game of My Life, p. 34.

81   "Nobody from my county . . . counting on you at 'Bama.": Dooley,
Game of My Life, p. 36.

81   When Brantley told Hallman . . . when I talked to him,": Dooley,
Game of My Life, p. 36.

82   "We've been snakebit something awful,": Cohen, p. 87.

82   All-world receiver Carlos . . . when we do, watch out.": Cohen, p. 87.

82   But the Gators surprised . . . FSU quarterback Gary Huff.: Cohen,
p. 87.

83   "All you do is run," . . . when they see how hot it is here,": Danny
Klein, "Practice Conditions Intense for Gators," *The Independent Florida Alligator*, Sept. 4, 2007, http:www.alligator.org/articles/2007/09/04/
sports/other_gator_sports/soccer.txt, Jan. 9, 2008.

84   They trailed 10-7 . . . in the third quarter: 17-7.: Robbie Andreu,
"Gators Stay Strong Through Deficit," *A Year for the Gators* (Gainesville: *The Gainesville Sun*, 2007), p. 33.

84   With 1:16 left in the third . . . team efforts I've ever seen.": Andreu
"Gators Stay Strong," p. 28.

84   You can recognize talent, . . . to recognize mental toughness.:
Sharpe, p. 48.

85   "the senior football player . . . leadership, character and courage.":
Florida 2007 Guide, p. 146.

85   who did the play-by-play . . . It was just superb.": Cohen, p. 35.

85   BC was a four-touchdown favorite: Cohen, p. 34.

85   Eight times in the last . . . inside the Gator 15.: Cohen, p. 35.

85   with just three minutes to play . . . quarterback on fourth down:
Cobb, p. 190.

85   Ferguson had five sacks . . . ten years later.: Cohen, p. 35.

86   "People were talking . . . took that personally.": Kevin Brockway,
"National Champions, *Florida Gators: 2006 NCAA Champions* (Gainesville: *The Gainesville Sun*, 2006), p. 112.

86   During UCLA's semifinal win . . . instructions to his defenders.: Pat
Dooley, "Greatest Gators Ever," *Florida Gators: 2006 NCAA Champions*
(Gainesville: *The Gainesville Sun*, 2006), p. 118.

87   The team hopped aboard a boat . . . going off without a hitch.: Cohen,
p. 9.

87   The referees put a particularly Cuban spin . . . arrested the Florida
coach.: Cohen, p. 10.

87   He had part of a trial . . . and made for home.: Cohen, pp. 10-11.

88   You could hear a pin drop.": Pat Dooley, "Dooley Book Excerpts:
The Start of Fine Careers as UF QBs," *gainesvillesun.com*, http://www.

gainesvillesun.com/article/20070901/NEWS/70901014, Jan. 2, 2008.

88   Coach Doug Dickey surprised . . . "Don, you got it.": Dooley, "Dooley Book Excerpts."

88   He had called his dad . . . little conviction that he'd be starting.: Dooley, "Dooley Book Excerpts."

88   Running back Nat Moore walked . . . what we've been waiting for.": Dooley, "Dooley Book Excerpts."

89   "propelled a once lackluster program into the epitome of excellence.": "Mary Wise," 2007 Volleyball Media Guide, p. 45, http://www.gatorzone.com/volleyball/media.

89   smashing the previous NCAA record by 36 games.: "Mary Wise."

90   The 45 points were the most . . . had given up in 26 years.: Wuerffel, p. 130.

90   Linebacker James Bates recalled . . . Gators were going crazy.": Kerasotis, p. 151.

90   the largest margin of victory against the No. one-ranked team in bowl history.: Kerasotis, p. 153.

90   "an unbelievable set of circumstances": Wuerffel, p. 129.

BIBLIOGRAPHY

Andreu, Robbie. "Florida's Blockbuster Play." The Gainesville Sun. 6 Nov. 2007. http://www.gainesvillesun.com/article/20071106/NEWS/711060308.

---. "Gators Make Most of Chances." A Year for the Gators: Florida Gators 2006 BCS National Champions. Gainesville: The Gainesville Sun, 2007. 114-119.

---. "Gators Stay Strong Through Deficit." A Year for the Gators: Florida Gators 2006 BCS National Champions. Gainesville: The Gainesville Sun, 2007. 28-33.

---. "Leak Nearly Flawless." A Year for the Gators: Florida Gators 2006 BCS National Champions. Gainesville: The Gainesville Sun, 2007. 18-23.

---. "Team Tebow." The Gainesville Sun. 9 Dec. 2007. http://www.gainesvillesun.com/article/20071210/NEWS/71209024.

---. "Spurrier's Return a Losing One." A Year for the Gators: Florida Gators 2006 BCS National Champions. Gainesville: The Gainesville Sun, 2007. 80-85.

---. "UF Strength Coach Marotti Teaches Players

Chemistry." *The Gainesville Sun.* 7 June 2008. http://www.gaines-ville.com/article/20080607/NEWS/599210388.

Bolton, Clyde. *The Crimson Tide: A Story of Alabama Football.* Huntsville, AL: The Strode Publishers, 1972.

---. *War Eagle: A Story of Auburn Football.* Huntsville, AL: The Strode Publishers, 1973.

"Break from Game Beneficial for UF's McGinnis." *The Gainesville Sun.* 10 Oct. 2007. http://www.gainesville.com/article/20071010/NEWS/71010006.

Brockway, Kevin. "#13 Joakim Noah." *Florida Gators: 2006 NCAA Champions.* Gainesville: *The Gainesville Sun,* 2006. 28.

---. "National Champions." *Florida Gators: 2006 NCAA Champions.* Gainesville: *The Gainesville Sun,* 2006, 112-117.

---. "Thanks for the Memories: Fans Honor Team, Offer Well Wishes." *The Gainesville Sun.* 7 April 2007. http://www.gainesville.com/article/20070407/SUNFRONT/704070340.

---. "Tourney Two-Peat." *Florida Gators: 2006 NCAA Champions.* Gainesville: *The Gainesville Sun,* 2006. 68-73.

Browning, Al. *Chomp 'em Gators: A Fun Look at University of Florida Football History.* Sterrett, AL: Colonial BancGroup, 2001.

Cobb, Arthur. *Go Gators! Official History: University of Florida Football: 1889-1966.* Pensacola: Sunshine Publishing Co., 1966.

Cohen, Marty. *Gator Tales: Stories, Stats and Stuff about Florida Football.* Wichita, KS: The Wichita Eagle and Beacon Publishing Co., 1995.

Culpepper, R. Alan. "The Gospel of Luke: Introduction, Commentary, and Reflections." *The New Interpreter's Bible.* Vol. IX. Nashville, TN: Abingdon Press, 1995. 1-490.

Dooley, Pat. "#2 Corey Brewer." *Florida Gators: 2006 NCAA Champions.* Gainesville: *The Gainesville Sun,* 2006. 100-01.

---. "Dooley Book Excerpts: The Start of Fine Careers as UF QBs." *gainesvillesun.com.* http://www.gainesvillesun.com/artcle/20070901/NEWS/70901014.

---. "Fake Punt Sunk [*sic*] Rebels' Chances." *The Gainesville Sun.* 22 Sept. 2007. http://www.gainesville.com/article/20070922/NEWS/70922013.

---. *Game of My Life: Florida: Memorable Stories of Gators Football.* Champaign, IL: Sports Publishing L.L.C., 2007.

---. "Greatest Gators Ever." *Florida Gators: 2006 NCAA Champions.* Gainesville: *The Gainesville Sun,* 2006. 118-121.

---. "Higgins Is Florida's 'Rudy.'" *A Year for the Gators: Florida Gators 2006 BCS National Champions.* Gainesville: *The Gainesville Sun,*

2007. 93-94.

---. "Waleszonia Reaches Goal Without Her Biggest Supporter." *The Gainesville Sun*. 28 May 2008. http://www.gainesville.com/ article/20080528/COLUMNISTS/141001047/1044.

Feinstein, John. "After a Change of Heart, Donovan Feels Right at Home." *The Washington Post*. 8 March 2008. http://www.washingtonpost.com/wp-dyn/content/article/2008/03/08.

Florida 2007 Guide. http://www.gatorzone.com/football/media/2007/pdf.

Kerasotis, Peter. *Stadium Stories: Florida Gators*. Guilford, CN: The Globe Pequot Press, 2005.

Klein, Danny. "Practice Conditions Intense for Gators." *The Independent Florida Alligator*. 4 Sept. 2007. http://www.alligator.org/ articles/2007/09/04/sports/other_gator_sports/soccer.txt.

---. "Tough Defense Leads UF Soccer." *The Independent Florida Alligator*. 20 Sept. 2007. http://www.alligator.org/articles/2007/09/20/sports/ other_gator_sports/asoccer.txt.

Litsky, Frank. "Charley Pell Is Dead at 60; Ousted as Florida Coach." *The New York Times*. 31 May 2001. http://query.nytimes.com/gst/ fullpage.html.

MacArthur, John. *Twelve Ordinary Men*. Nashville, TN: W Publishing Group, 2002.

"Mary Wise." *2007 Volleyball Media Guide*. 45-46. http://www.gatorzone. com/volleyball/media.

Murphy, Austin. "Tim Tebow." *Sports Illustrated Presents Florida Gators: How Florida Won its Second National Title in Three Seasons*. 14 Jan. 09. 55-58.

"No Panic, Gators Just Come up Clutch." *The Gainesville Sun*. 23 March 2007. http://www.gainesville.com/article/20070323/COLUMNISTS/70323035.

"The Pride of the Sunshine." *Wikipedia, the free encyclopedia*. http:// en.wikipedia.org/wiki/The_Pride_of_the_Sunshine.

Reinink, Mary. "Gators Go for Glory." *The Gainesville Sun*. 31 March 2007. http://www.gainesville.com/article/20070331/LOCAL/703310355.

"Rhonda Faehn, Head Coach." *Florida Gymnastics 2008*. http://www. gatorzone.com/gymnastics/media/2008/pdf/staff/faehn.pdf.

Richardson, Suzy A. "Coaching Character." *The Gainesville Sun*. 7 Oct. 2007. http://www.gainesville.com/article/20071007/ NEWS/710060317.

Sharpe, Wilton. *Gators Glory: Great Eras in Florida Football*. Nashville, TN: Cumberland House Publishing, Inc.,

2007.

Staples. Andy. "Taking the Bite out of the Dawgs." *Sports Illustrated Presents Florida Gators: How Florida Won Its Second National Title in Three Seasons.* 14 Jan. 09. 27.

"Steve Spurrier." *Wikipedia, the free encyclopedia.* http://en.wikipedia.org/wiki/Steve_Spurrier.

Thomsen, Ian. "Swamped." *Sports Illustrated.* 27 Sept. 1999. http://vault.sportsillustrated.cnn.com/vault/article/magazine/MAG1017130/index.htm.

Wahl, Grant. "The Gators Again." *Sports Illustrated.* 9 April 2007. http://vault.sportsillustrated.ccn.com/vault/article/magazine/MAG1104568/2/index.htm.

Wuerffel, Danny with Mike Bianchi. *Tales from the Gator Swamp: Reflections of Faith and Football.* Champaign, IL: Sports Publishing L.L.C., 2006.

Zimmerman, Brandon. "15-Year-Old Takes on UF, Golf." *The Gainesville Sun.* 11 Feb. 2008. http://www.gainesville.com/article/20080211/NEWS/802110319.

---. "Breakfast Club Helps UF Players Pack Pounds." *The Gainesville Sun.* 25 Sept. 2007. http://www.gainesvillesun.com/article/20070925/NEWS/709250316.

---. "Emergency Appendectomy Just Not Enough to Stop UF's Mullen." *The Gainesville Sun.* 2 Oct. 2007. http://www.gainesville.com/article/20071002/NEWS/710020325.

---. "Faehn Returns with Gators No. 1." *The Gainesville Sun.* 15 Jan. 2008. http://www/gainesville.com/article/20080115/NEWS/212524708.

---. "Gators Take Their Time to Beat UK." *The Gainesville Sun.* 22 April 2007. http://www.gainesville.com/article/20070422/GATORS04/70422008.

---. "Gators Track Coach Tom Jones Dies at 62." *The Gainesville Sun,* 22 March 2007. http://www.gainesville.com/article/20070322/GATORS14/703220375.

---. "Sinclair Perfect in Florida's Win." *The Gainesville Sun.* 3 March 2007. http://www.gainesville.com/article/20070303/GATORS18/703030313.

---. "Thompson Had Long Journey Home." *The Gainesville Sun.* 30 Jan. 2008. http://www.gatorsports.com/article/20080130/NEWS/4456524/1016.

---. "UF Volleyball's Hampton Lives out Her Dream." *The Gainesville Sun.* 18 Nov. 2007. http://www.gatorsports.com/article/20071118/NEWS/71118002.

---. "UF Walks off with Monster Rally." *The Gainesville Sun*. 7 April 2007. http://www.gainesville.com/article/20070407/GATORS04/70407012.

---. "'We Were Honored You Were Our Coach.'" *The Gainesville Sun*. 28 March 2007. http://www.gainesville.com/article/20070328/GA-TORS14/70328007.

INDEX
(LAST NAME, DEVOTION DAY NUMBER)